PROBLEMS OF POLITICAL PHILOSOPHY

PROBLEMS OF POLITICAL PHILOSOPHY

D. D. RAPHAEL

PRAEGER PUBLISHERS
New York · Washington · London

Praeger Publishers, Inc.
111 Fourth Avenue, New York, N.Y. 10003, U.S.A.
5 Cromwell Place, London, SW7, England

Published in the United States of America in 1970
by Praeger Publishers, Inc.

© 1970 BY PALL MALL PRESS LTD, LONDON, ENGLAND

All rights reserved

LIBRARY OF CONGRESS CATALOG CARD NUMBER: 76–95688

Printed in Great Britain

CONTENTS

PREFACE

This book is intended to introduce students to the problems (not the history) of political philosophy without presupposing any previous knowledge of philosophy. A relatively short introduction must leave many things half-said and others not said at all. The first chapter is one man's picture of the subject, not a programme for what follows. In what does follow there is inevitable selection and limitation, most apparent perhaps on the topic of democracy, adequate discussion of which would need a book to itself.

Chapters I–IV were written in the second of two terms which I spent as a Visiting Fellow of All Souls College, Oxford, and I wish to record my gratitude to the Warden and Fellows for the opportunity of full-time scholarly work in beautiful and peaceful surroundings. The difference it made may be judged from a comparison: Chapters I–IV were completed at All Souls in six weeks; the writing of Chapters V–VIII amid the press of my usual administrative and teaching responsibilities at Glasgow stretched over ten months.

I wish to express my thanks also to Mr. Michael Lessnoff, who read the book in typescript and made a number of valuable criticisms; Mr. J. C. Rees, who gave me some comments on the first chapter; and Miss Anne S. Hutton, who typed the work and re-read the proofs with her customary efficiency.

Parts of Chapter VI, Sections 1 and 3, together with a little of Chapter III, Section 3, are a revised version of an article entitled 'Equality, Democracy, and International Law', which has previously been published in NOMOS IX, *Equality*.

Glasgow 1969   D.D.R.

I WHAT IS POLITICAL PHILOSOPHY?

1 SCIENTIFIC THEORY AND PHILOSOPHICAL THEORY

The terms 'political theory' and 'political philosophy' are often used interchangeably, but there is a recognizable difference between the theoretical work of political scientists and that of political philosophers. Similarly there is a recognizable difference between sociological theory, as pursued by theoretically-minded sociologists, and social philosophy. In discussing the difference between the two types of theory, it will be useful to consider the social and the political together. There is of course a distinction between the social and the political, but my initial purpose is to distinguish philosophical theorizing about society and the State from the kind of theorizing that is done by some political scientists and sociologists.

A definition of 'politics', or of what can be described as 'political', is the subject of controversy and will be considered in Chapter II, Section 1. For the moment it is more relevant to note that the idea of 'social' studies can be used in a wider or in a narrower sense. In the wider sense, social studies include the study of politics, embracing everything that has to do with the activities of men in society; much sociological theory is of this character. In the narrower sense, social or sociological studies are confined to those areas of social activity that do not form the subject-matter of other, more definitely circumscribed, social sciences, such as political science or economics; into this category come sociological studies of the family, or of religion as a social institution, or of educational institutions. Usually, when speaking of social or sociological theory, and still more when speaking of social philosophy, one is using the term 'social' in the wider and not in the narrower sense. Social philosophy is of broader scope than political philosophy and can indeed be said to include it. Likewise social or sociological theory is of broader scope than the theory of political science.

Social and political theory as pursued by sociologists and political scientists is theory in the scientific sense of the term. Its aim is explanation. The social sciences, like the natural sciences (i.e. the physical and biological sciences), do not merely record individual facts but seek to explain them as instances of general laws, and the attempt to provide such general explanatory laws constitutes the theoretical aspect of a science. Up to now, sociology and political science have not been as successful as economics in establishing explanatory laws, but many interesting hypotheses have been put forward as candidates for the status of explanatory laws, and these hypotheses can be tested in the same way as the hypotheses of natural science. Recent work along these lines has taken the form of providing sophisticated 'models' of group behaviour, but for the purposes of elementary illustration it will suffice to mention some older and well-known generalizations. One example is Karl Marx's theory that a change from one form of society to another is always the result of class struggle, which in turn is ultimately due to changes in the 'forces of production', i.e. in the materials or tools or type of labour used to produce goods. Another example is Robert Michels' 'iron law of oligarchy', the thesis that any organization, including those that begin democratically, must end up under the control of a small group. A third example, this time from the sociology of law, is Sir Henry Maine's generalization that the legal systems of progressive societies move from the idea of status to that of contract. A still narrower hypothesis, taken from the field of political science, is the suggestion that a multi-party political system leads to unstable government. It may be that none of these hypotheses is a genuine explanatory law, but this is what they aim to be, generalizations based on facts of experience and serving to explain further such facts. The generalizations are formed and are tested in the same way as hypotheses in the natural sciences. They rest on the evidence of factual instances, and they can be disproved by pointing to other instances which do not conform to them.

Social and political philosophy is different, but in what way? It is often said that social and political philosophy, as practised in the past by traditional philosophers, differs from the scientific type of theory in being 'normative' instead of 'positive'. What is meant by this is that scientific theory deals with positive facts, with what is in fact the case, while the philosophical kind of 'theory' is really a doctrine, or an 'ideology', setting up 'norms' or ideal standards for society and government, telling us what ought to be the case, or what we ought to do. A prime example is Plato's *Republic*, which depicts an ideal society or utopia. I myself think that this view of traditional political philosophy is questionable. It is true that some of the classical political philosophers have set out ideal forms of society, but in my opinion this has not been their central concern. Even in Plato, the purpose of depicting an ideal society is to criticize existing society and to promote understanding of general social concepts such as justice. Social and political philosophy can be regarded as normative in a less obvious way, but first I must describe what it does.

Social and political philosophy is of course a branch of philosophy; it is an application of philosophical thinking to ideas about society and the State. Philosophy has taken many different forms, but I find it useful to interpret the main tradition of western philosophy as having had two connected aims: (a) the clarification of concepts, for the purpose of (b) the critical evaluation of beliefs. In explaining these two aims of traditional philosophy, I shall deal first with (b), since that, in my opinion, has been the basic aim, whether or not it can in fact be fulfilled. In traditional philosophy, aim (a), the clarification of concepts, has been subsidiary and was pursued only as a necessary aid to the basic aim of evaluating beliefs; but in the philosophy of the present day, aim (*a*) is paramount and is often pursued for its own sake.

2 CRITICAL EVALUATION OF BELIEFS

On the interpretation of traditional philosophy that I am putting forward, its fundamental purpose has been the critical evaluation of beliefs, the attempt to give rational grounds for accepting or rejecting beliefs which we normally take for granted without thinking of any grounds for justification. Philosophy differs from science in that science seeks explanation while philosophy seeks justification. The word 'justification' can, however, be misleading if one takes it to mean positive justification only. One is then led to suppose that traditional philosophy must be conservative, always attempting to defend old ideas in the face of new ones that would upset the existing order. This of course is not true. Sceptical philosophy has been at least as common as conservative. I use the word 'justification' to mean the giving of rational or justifying grounds either for accepting a belief or for rejecting it.

This procedure naturally has an important place in science too, as it must have in any enterprise that sets out to be rational. When a scientist adduces evidence and logical argument for or against a hypothesis, he is presenting rational grounds for accepting the hypothesis as true or rejecting it as false. His work differs from that of the philosopher in the character of the hypothesis itself, which usually takes the form of a causal explanation. The scientist seeks causes; and in that quest, because his enterprise is a rational one, unlike the irrational positing of causes in superstition, he also seeks justifying reasons. The philosopher is not specially concerned with causal explanation (except when he turns his interest to the procedure of science itself in order to understand its character), and is not specially qualified, as those versed in a particular science are, to offer causal explanations. The philosopher is ready to inquire into rational grounds for or against any kind of belief, not just beliefs about causes.

This is not to say that philosophers in fact turn their attention to any and every belief at any and every time. Philosophical problems about particular kinds of belief arise from historical circumstances. The need to seek rational grounds usually arises when something has happened to make us doubt the validity of a belief that has previously been taken for granted, and this something has usually been a new belief that appears to be incompatible with the old one. For example, the emergence of modern science appeared to challenge the validity of certain traditional religious beliefs. The Copernican theory of the solar system was incompatible with the idea, apparently attested by common-sense observation and by the cosmology of Genesis, that the earth is fixed and that the sun and moon move around it. Again, the Darwinian theory of evolution by natural selection was inconsistent with the Biblical account of creation.

The new scientific theories were based upon rational methods that commanded the respect of those who understood them. Since the new theories appeared to conflict with traditional beliefs, the demands of consistency required one of three possibilities:

(1) The traditional beliefs could be discarded as myth, based on imagination or limited evidence.

(2) The new beliefs could be rejected, on the ground that the evidence for them was less reliable than that of scriptural revelation.

(3) One or other of the two sets of beliefs could be modified so as to make them compatible with each other.

The second course was taken by diehards, but it could not last for long, since the claims of the new beliefs were rationally convincing. Hence the first and the third possibilities have won out.

It is here that the philosophy of knowledge (commonly called epistemology and metaphysics) has played its part. In the first place, philosophers have tried to bring out clearly the underlying implications of the two sets of beliefs, so as to show just where the incompatibility lies. Secondly, philosophers have then recommended ways of resolving the incompatibility, and these have taken the form either of method (1) or of method (3).

Method (1) produces iconoclastic or sceptical philosophy—sceptical, that is to say, in relation to traditional or common-sense beliefs, for although scepticism of this kind can then lead to a more generalized scepticism, total scepticism has in fact been rare and a *jeu d'esprit*. Other philosophers have pursued method (3) and have been led to suggest new ways of looking at the data, new conceptual schemes, i.e. new frames of ideas for fitting on *all* the relevant facts, so as to produce consistency; a consequence of this has been a modified version of either the old beliefs, or of the new, or of both.

A parallel process occurs in the philosophy of practice (moral, social, and political philosophy). This is concerned, not with beliefs about what is *true*, but with beliefs or principles about what is *right* or *good*, for man and society. Traditional principles of right and wrong, good and evil, come to be questioned in the face of new knowledge, such as the knowledge that different societies have different rules, or new scientific knowledge about the causes or effects of some modes of behaviour. For example, when the Greek Sophists travelled to non-Greek lands and found different customs and moral rules in different societies, they were led to question the supposed natural or absolute character of moral principles; in consequence they asked themselves which rules, if any, were *really* right, or was there nothing to choose between them. Again, advances in psychology have shown that some kinds of socially harmful behaviour on the part of certain individuals are determined by pathological abnormalities and are better treated as illness than as crime; this leads one to ask how far the reinterpretation of such behaviour should be carried, and whether our usual ideas of crime and responsibility, and indeed more generally of moral and immoral conduct, need to be revised. When such questioning occurs, the philosopher tries to consider how far, and on what grounds, the traditional ideas, and the new ones, can be rationally justified. As in the philosophy of knowledge, he tries to bring out the underlying implications of the old and the new, to locate the precise points at which there is inconsistency, and to resolve the inconsistencies either by rejecting the old beliefs or by proposing a revised conceptual framework which will accommodate all the data but with a modification of either or both of the conflicting sets of ideas.

That, as I see it, has been the primary task of traditional philosophy, whether in the field of knowledge or in that of action. Of course, once a problem has been raised and has been met by the propounding of a new conceptual framework or 'system of philosophy', other thinkers are liable to turn their attention to that system itself. Philosophy lives by constant criticism. It arises from doubt and criticism of existing ideas, and it remains vigorous and healthy only if it is self-critical also. So the emergence of a new philosophical schema, in answer to a problem that first arose outside philosophy, tends to produce a circle of philosophical discussion about that schema itself, as well as about the problem which produced it. As in science, an inquiry which originated in external needs will then be pursued for its own sake. The philosophical schema of one thinker will be revised by others or succeeded by a different type of schema which avoids the defects of the first. In the course of this progression of philosophical discussion, the original external problem is sometimes forgotten, or else it is treated as still an intellectual problem when the doubts and difficulties of real life that first produced it have long been resolved; and then philosophical inquiry seems to the man in the street an arid waste of time on things that do not matter; it has degenerated into an intellectual exercise that interests only a small coterie of initiates. But in time there is liable to arise some new problem which, like the original one, really does disturb long-standing beliefs that we carry about with us and use in our daily life, and then a new philosophical movement appears.

My account of the primary aim of traditional philosophy is an individual interpretation, but I think a good many philosophers might agree that it is a fair description of one important function of philosophy in the past. Now this aim of traditional philosophy has come to be mistrusted for the following reason. If a belief is to be rationally justified, it must satisfy two criteria. The first is consistency, and the means of testing this is logic, the chief tool of the philosopher. But consistency alone is not enough to make a belief, or set of beliefs, rationally acceptable.

Suppose we have two or more sets of beliefs, each of which is internally consistent, but which are inconsistent at some points with each other, like alternative systems of geometry. How are we to know which of them ought to be accepted? We therefore need a second criterion. In the case of beliefs about matters of fact, we need to know which of the internally consistent alternatives is true, i.e. which applies to, or accords with, the actual facts of the world. While philosophers are well qualified to test consistency, they are in no special position to say what the relevant facts are. Their specialty is clear thinking, not factual investigation. Orderly investigation of facts is the business of science. Therefore many philosophers to-day maintain that it is for science to say whether a belief is true or false; and if a particular belief is such that no scientific investigation of it is possible, either as yet or in principle, then we must not ask whether it is true or false. The philosophy of knowledge cannot in either event determine whether a belief passes the second test of accordance with fact.

With the subject-matter of the philosophy of practice (moral, social, and political philosophy) the difficulty is even greater. The first criterion, of consistency, can again be used by the philosopher. But in this instance it is not clear what is to take the place of the second criterion of accordance with facts. It is not a question of determining what is true or false, but one of determining what is right or wrong, good or bad. Values are not facts in the ordinary sense of the word; and if there is a sense in which values can be treated as facts, there is no recognized procedure for deciding which among conflicting sets of values is to be regarded as factual or objective. There is no science which can tell us this, and it is hard to say what other kind of investigation could do so. If, for example, different people have different, and incompatible, ideas of what would be a just order of society, how are we to decide which is correct? Or if some countries adopt democratic principles, while others adopt communist principles which appear to be incompatible at some points with the democratic, how are we to argue rationally in favour of the one as against the other?

I myself think that it *is* possible to do something about this problem, or at least that there are lines of inquiry which are still worth pursuing. Since the difficulty is especially acute with the philosophy of practice, and since my major concern in this book is with political philosophy, I shall confine myself to the latter in outlining my reply to the criticism of the traditional aim. The criticism, in my opinion, underrates what can be done negatively to *disprove* a set of principles. That is to say, critical evaluation has to take the form, not of directly justifying one belief, but of indirectly supporting it by the elimination of alternatives.

In the first place, the criticism underrates the extent to which the criterion of consistency can be conclusive as a negative test. It is often possible to disclose inconsistency in a set of political ideas, thereby showing that, in its existing form at least, it should be rejected as irrational. Take as an example the conflict between democratic and Nazi principles. Some philosophers said in the 1930s that there was no way of arguing rationally against Nazi ideas; you just had to take your choice, depending no doubt on your feelings and what you were used to. This is not true of everything that the Nazis believed. They held, for example, that one group of human beings, the 'Aryan race', was superior to other human groups, the 'non-Aryan races'. This is the sort of ideological belief that is supposed to be immune from rational refutation. But Nazi doctrine went on to refer to 'non-Aryans' as 'sub-human', in order to justify the view that 'non-Aryans' were inferior to 'Aryans'. In suggesting that 'non-Aryans' were inferior because they were less than human, the Nazis implied that all *human* beings were on the higher level of value, and this of course was inconsistent with the claim that one group of human beings was of higher value than other human beings. The underlying implication of their use of the term 'sub-human' shows that at heart they shared the view of democrats that it is wrong to place different groups of human beings on different levels of value.

It must not be supposed that the use of this criterion always favours democratic beliefs. Inconsistencies may be found within democratic ideas too. Some people think, for example, that there is an inconsistency between the pursuit of liberty and that of equality, each of which is a principle of democratic thought. If these two ends are in fact inconsistent, the demands of reason require that we should abandon or modify at least one of them.

Secondly, the criticism of traditional political philosophy neglects the part that facts do play in the support of value-judgements. Although judgements of value cannot be *directly* tested by the criterion of accordance with fact, they are sus-ceptible to an *indirect* test of this kind, for they often presuppose beliefs about facts which can be subjected to the test of accordance. It is true that philosophers are in no special position to discover facts, but they can make use of facts which have been established by scientists or which are attested by common observation, in order to show that a political principle depends on factual assumptions which are false. I again take as an example the Nazi doctrine about the superiority of the 'Aryan race'. This presupposes that there is such a thing as an Aryan *race* in the biological sense of the term; and we can use data from the sciences of ethnology and philology to show that this factual presupposition is false and that the only sound distinction be-tween 'Aryan' and 'non-Aryan' relates to languages. If there is no such thing as an Aryan race, any judgements about the Aryan race, be they judgements of fact or judgements of value, have no genuine application. This kind of argument of course does not prove that different groups of people are of equal value, but it removes a prop that was used to support the Nazi doctrine and thereby helps to discredit that doctrine. Again, we can sometimes disprove a political doctrine by showing that it rests on factual assumptions which are known to be false from the familiar daily experience of everyone, not just of scientists or of philosophers. Some important political doctrines presuppose that human beings are motivated only by self-interest, and a relevant comparison of political authority with authority in some other forms of social organization, a family, a church, a school, can easily show that the presupposition is mistaken and that it has acquired plausibility only because attention has been confined to certain areas of behaviour and authority.

It is no defect in philosophy that the progress of critical evaluation should depend on negative refutation rather than on positive establishment of beliefs. Science too progresses by the disproof of false hypotheses rather than by the direct proof of those that are taken to be true. I do not wish to suggest, however, that all the problems of critical evaluation in political philosophy can be solved in this way. A conflict between two sets of political principles, e.g. between the principles of liberal democracy and those of communism, or between the principles of the Conservative and Labour Parties in Britain, often rests on the balancing of two or more ideals and the comparative rating given to each; it may be a question of how we rate liberty against fraternity or equality. In considering the rival claims in such a conflict, the philosophical methods of showing up inconsistency or false factual presuppositions are apt to leave unresolved the central issue of disagreement on comparative value. Nevertheless those methods can be effective for some of the problems of political philosophy.

At any rate, the point of critical evaluation, if it is practicable, will be clear enough. I turn now to the second function of philosophy.

3 CLARIFICATION OF CONCEPTS

According to my interpretation of traditional philosophy, the clarification of concepts has traditionally been undertaken as a subsidiary function serving the primary aim of evaluating beliefs. In order to know whether a belief is tenable, and in particular whether it involves any inconsistencies, either within itself or between it and other accepted beliefs, it is necessary to understand just what the belief is and what it implies. We need to know clearly what is meant by the terms used in it. Consequently a good deal of philosophy is concerned with the meaning of general ideas or concepts. Those philosophers of the present day who consider that the critical evaluation of beliefs is a misguided or impracticable pursuit for philosophy, also hold that the clarification of concepts is the sole task that philosophy can successfully perform. For them, therefore, this is no longer a subsidiary function but the central business of philosophy. Whether or not it is the only job that philosophy can usefully do, it occupies the main part of much philosophical inquiry, and it will occupy the main part of what I have to say in this book.

A concept is a general idea or notion that applies to a number of things. It is often helpful to think of concepts as the uses of general words. At any rate the examination of concepts can only be carried out by considering the uses of words. When I speak of 'general words' I mean words that refer to a number of things, by contrast with names, which are intended to identify individual things. Sometimes names fail to identify. I once asked an American woman student, at a philosophy course, what was her name, and thought she was pulling my leg when she replied 'Socrates'; she was in fact of Greek origin and was called Persephone Socrates. But at any rate in that group the name 'Persephone Socrates' referred to one person only, while the general term 'student' applied both to her and to all her colleagues. There is no difficulty in understanding what is meant by 'student' or by most other general words. Philosophical problems are usually concerned with concepts that are *very* general, like the concept of a person, of mind, matter, space, time. Many of the ideas of social and political thought, such as the concept of society, of authority, social class, justice, liberty, democracy, are not only highly general but also vague.

In trying to clarify general ideas, philosophy has three related purposes, analysis, synthesis, and improvement of concepts. By analysis of a concept I mean specifying its elements, often by way of definition; for example, one can analyse or define sovereignty as supreme legal authority, specifying the three essential elements which make up the concept. By synthesis of concepts I mean showing the logical relationships whereby one concept implies or is implied by another; for example, one can show a logical relationship between the concept of a right and that of an obligation by pointing out that whenever A has a right against B, this implies that B has an obligation. By improvement of a concept I mean recommending a definition or use that will assist clarity or coherence; for example, one can recommend, as I do, that the concept of sovereignty should be used *only* of the legal authority, and not of the coercive power, of a State.

The three tasks of analysis, synthesis, and improvement go together. In order to analyse or define a concept, you often, if not always, have to note implications, logical relations. To take a simple example for purposes of illustration: if you define 'man' as a rational animal, you are not only distinguishing two elements of the concept, being rational and being an animal; you are also subsuming a species under a genus and differentiating it from other species. Consequently you can make the simple inference: if anything is a man, it must be an animal. You have the beginnings of a little pattern of synthesis or logical system, which can be pictured as the inclusion of one class of things, men, among the wider class, animals, or else as the branching out of the general idea, animal, into two divisions, rational and non-rational, the first division comprising men and the second all other animals. You are also improving, or at any rate refining, the concept of man as compared with its use in ordinary life; for when we normally use the word 'man' in an everyday context, we are not thinking explicitly of the idea of a rational animal, or of a class of animals that excludes elephants, emus, and echinoderms.

Many modern philosophers would reject the improvement of concepts as a proper purpose of philosophy, just as they would reject the critical evaluation of beliefs, and for the same sort of reason, namely that it is not the business of philosophy to decide what is better or worse, or to say that a change in the use of an idea would be an improvement. I think this is because these philosophers are usually more interested in the philosophy of knowledge than in the philosophy of practice. The concepts that are studied in the philosophy of knowledge tend to change slowly, or in some instances perhaps not at all, and such changes as do occur are usually the result of scientific advance. It is therefore resonable enough, at first sight, to say that a philosopher is not specially qualified to recommend the improvement of a concept;

his task is to elucidate the ways in which it is commonly used or the significance of a change that has already come about as a result of scientific progress. (I say it is reasonable 'at first sight', because I think that in fact this view of the philosopher's function should be qualified even for the philosophy of knowledge.)

The thesis, however, is less plausible with some of the concepts studied in the philosophy of practice, and especially in social and political philosophy. In many tribal and peasant societies of the past, social institutions and the ideas that go along with them have remained relatively stable over a long period. But societies that engender philosophical reflection on their structure and on the ideas associated with it are societies which are subject to quite perceptible change, and this is liable to lead to changes in the meaning of some of the ideas. For example, the ideas of 'justice' and 'merit' or 'worth' do not have the same meaning in the literature of fifth-century Athens as they have in the Homeric poems relating to an earlier, aristocratic, form of Greek society. On the other hand, although Athenian democracy was in certain respects more democratic than modern democracies, the Athenians' concept of justice included little or nothing of an explicit notion of the 'rights' of the individual, a notion which plays a large part in modern social and political thought. In our own time we can see not only that the scope of application of this notion is being widened, but that its meaning is to some extent being modified. A philosopher may think that his task is simply to chart the old and the new meanings, but it seems to me that the process of clarification must often inevitably carry with it a sharpening, and so a slight change, of the meaning of the concept as habitually employed.

The point of the primary aim of traditional philosophy, the critical evaluation of beliefs, was plain enough—provided that the aim could be realized. If the secondary aim, the clarification of concepts, is pursued in the service of evaluating beliefs, its point likewise will be apparent. Thus, for example, if we want to consider possible methods of justifying a preference for democracy over its rivals, we need to know clearly what is meant by the concept of democracy and by such concepts as liberty and equality, which are commonly taken to be an essential part of democratic doctrine. But if, as many philosophers think nowadays, the evaluation of beliefs is impracticable, what is the point of going on with the clarification of concepts?

I must leave it to others to defend the antics of philosophy in general when confined to the analysis of concepts. So far as social and political philosophy is concerned, it is not hard to justify a purely conceptual treatment. We all use terms like 'democracy', 'freedom', 'social justice', and nowadays 'the Welfare State'. We have a rough idea of what we mean, and more often than not we have no difficulty in understanding these terms when used by others; e.g. by a democracy we may mean a State in which the rulers are chosen by popular election. But then we are liable to contrast a democratic with a totalitarian State; and so we may be a little puzzled when we find communist countries calling themselves 'people's democracies'. We are inclined to ask: 'Isn't our democracy too a democracy of the people? What on earth do those communists mean by distinguishing their form of government as a "people's democracy"? They don't sound as if they had their tongue in their cheek.' Or again, suppose you were to hear, as I have heard, New Zealanders saying that the British system of university education is 'undemocratic'. Well, in a way, we see what they mean; or at least we see it if we know that university education in New Zealand is open to a wider section of the population than ours is. But then we may reflect: 'Democracy surely relates to government, to the fact that every adult has a vote, not to education. Why does the New Zealander say "undemocratic" when he means "unequalitarian"? Yet, on the other hand, democracy does have something to do with equality; but what exactly?' Already we have begun to try to analyse the concept of democracy, and to consider its logical relation to the concept of equality. We have begun, in a small way, to think philosophically about a political concept.

Here is another example. The history of political philosophy since the sixteenth century contains a good deal of tedious-looking discussion about the concept of sovereignty. Much of it is indeed tedious enough. Yet there are important historical reasons why philosophers of the sixteenth and seventeenth centuries should have placed the idea of sovereignty in the forefront of their thought; and further historical development has now made this concept a part of our intellectual and linguistic equipment for discussing some questions of politics. You will often find, in political discussion about joining an international or supra-national organization such as the European Common Market, that people talk about 'giving up our sovereignty' and debating whether we should or should not do so. Rightly or wrongly, this is regarded as an important issue, to be taken into account along with economic or with other political questions, when deciding whether Britain should try to join the European Common Market. Well, if we have no clear idea of what is meant by 'sovereignty', we simply do not know what we are talking about; our 'national sovereignty' becomes a sacred cow that must not be touched, and we have no idea *why* it should not be touched or what kind of animal it is anyway.

These are the sort of reasons why the clarification of concepts is worth doing for its own sake, even if one thinks that it cannot be used for the further purpose of evaluating beliefs. It is perhaps worth giving a word of warning that the results of a conceptual inquiry sometimes seem disappointingly meagre. The clarification of concepts is like cleaning the house. When you have cleaned the house, there is not much to be seen for your work. You have not acquired any new possessions, though you will have thrown out some things that are not wanted and are just a nuisance. What you have at the end of it is a tidier house, in which you can move around more easily and in which you can find things when you need them.

The analogy is apt in another respect also. Cleaning the house is not a job that can be done once and for all. You have to do it every week. The mere business of living continues to produce more rubbish, which has to be cleared regularly. Philosophy seems to go round and round the same old problems and to make no progress. This is in fact an illusion; progress is made, though it is gradual. The main point, however, is that philosophy is a mental clearance, not the acquisition of new information. The clearance needs to be done again in every generation with improved tools, the vacuum cleaner, so to speak, taking the place of the sweeping brush. And it needs to be done every so often in the life of an individual. If one feels, at the end of reading a particular work of philosophy, that a few things have been tidied up, one should not suppose that this is the end of the matter. In a few years' time one may well find that the earlier conclusions themselves need to be tidied up or even discarded. The chief thing that we should hope to acquire from the study of political philosophy is not a final answer to problems but the habit of careful thought. The distinctions made in the clarification of concepts are often simple enough, once they are understood, but the initial understanding may require time and effort. Yet it is well worth while. Without the simple distinctions of social and political philosophy, we are likely to talk and act confusedly in social and political affairs and are liable to follow blind alleys in social and political science.

4 PHILOSOPHY AND IDEOLOGY

Having stated what political philosophy is, I can now turn back to a question raised earlier, whether or in what sense political philosophy is normative. I said in Section 1 that traditional political philosophy is often described as being normative or ideological, setting up norms or ideal standards for society and government. This is supposed to be the main difference between political philosophy and political science, which is positive, explaining how governments in fact conduct their affairs and how men in fact behave in the pursuit of actual political objectives, instead of prescribing what governments ought to do and what ought to be our political objectives. The account of political philosophy which I have given also makes it normative but in a rather different way. In particular, my account does not imply that political philosophy is ideology, if ideology means, as it is usually taken to mean, a prescriptive doctrine that is not supported by rational argument.

The critical evaluation of beliefs is of course normative in that it evaluates; but by 'critical evaluation', as I have explained, I mean seeking rational grounds for accepting or rejecting beliefs, and in this respect philosophy is no more (and no less) normative than explanatory theory, whether in social or in natural science. When explanatory theory provides evidence (with or without supporting logical argument) for or against a hypothesis, it is giving us rational grounds for accepting the hypothesis as true or rejecting it as false. Critical evaluation in the philosophy of knowledge is doing the same thing, though usually relying more heavily on logical argument than on the presentation of factual evidence. The result of critical evaluation of a proposition in the philosophy of knowledge is to give us grounds for accepting the proposition as true or for rejecting it as false. The result of critical evaluation in the philosophy of practice is rather different. Instead of seeking rational grounds for accepting a proposition as worthy of assent (i.e. as being true), or for rejecting it as unworthy of assent (i.e. as being false), the philosophy of practice seeks rational grounds for accepting a proposition as worthy of being followed in action (i.e. as being right or what we ought to do), or for rejecting it as unworthy of being followed in action (i.e. as being wrong or what we ought not to do). Nevertheless, in the philosophy of practice, as in the philosophy of knowledge and in explanatory theory, the decision to accept or reject a proposition does not depend on emotive preference but on the presentation of reasons. I have already illustrated how the logical test of consistency and the empirical test of accordance with fact both have their place in the elimination of political doctrines as irrational.

There is ample scope for rational argument about judgements of value, and argument of the same kind as is used in the discussion of judgements of fact. I am far from suggesting that all disputes about value can be settled rationally, but it should not be supposed that rational argument has no place at all in the discussion of values. The point is that the *philosophical* discussion of values is a discussion by means of rational argument, and rational argument of the same kind as is used in the philosophy of knowledge and in scientific theory. It is normative, in that it aims to justify (to give reasons for) the acceptance or rejection of doctrines; but so are the philosophy of knowledge and scientific theory in aiming to justify (to give reasons for) the acceptance or rejection of beliefs about matters of fact. The subject of the positive or negative justification in the former instance is a judgement of value, and if one of two conflicting alternatives is successfully eliminated, this means that the philosophical inquiry can be said to have given support to the remaining value-judgement. But the fact that the better supported alternative is a value-judgement does not in itself add to or alter the normative character of the philosophical process. That process is normative only in the sense that it gives reasons for accepting or rejecting a proposition. The reasoning process in the philosophy of knowledge or in scientific theory does exactly the same thing and is normative in the same sense. Neither is ideological. A set of value-judgements which have not been subjected to rational scrutiny by the tests of consistency and accordance may be called ideological. The conclusions of political philosophy, as I have described it, cannot.

What of the clarification of concepts? Those who discard the primary function of traditional political philosophy on the ground that it is normative or ideological, would say the same of the improvement of concepts but not of analysis and synthesis; and therefore they practise the latter, usually under the name of 'analysis' alone, and claim that they do not suggest any improvement of the concepts they analyse. Plainly the improvement of concepts is normative, since it recommends certain usages or definitions. Analysis and synthesis are positive, in that they aim simply at making plain what is already the case. However, I think that it is hardly possible to pursue analysis and synthesis without at the same time suggesting some improvement of concepts. Even the simplest kind of analysis or definition, as in my trite example of defining man as a rational animal, tends to refine a concept, to pare off some of its associations and to bring into a clear light what is taken to be its essential meaning. As a result, the concept when analysed does not have quite the same meaning as it has in ordinary use. The very fact that it is now relatively clear, where before it was relatively vague or blurred, means that it has been refined. In social and political studies especially, the clarification of concepts is liable to include improvement of them. For the general concepts of social and political thought change with changes in the form of society, and the social philosopher, in the course of his analysis of concepts and his review of their history, can often see that concepts are undergoing an implicit change which he wants to make explicit. His clarification therefore presents us with something that is not quite the same as the concept actually in use at the time.

If I am right, the second aim of political philosophy, which is retained by those who discard the first aim, is also, in part, a normative pursuit. Like the critical evaluation of beliefs, however, it need not be ideological, i.e. non-rationally normative. I said in Section 3 that the improvement of concepts is pursued in the interests of clarity or coherence, and each of these is a rational objective. Coherence means either consistency or, more strongly, positive logical connection; and clarity is an aid to understanding and to the avoidance of intellectual confusion. Both of the traditional functions of political philosophy are normative, and neither is ideological.

5 METHODOLOGY OF THE SOCIAL SCIENCES

One should not try to make a rigid separation between social and political philosophy. Some of the time-honoured subjects of political philosophy, such as the nature of the State, sovereignty, and the grounds of political obligation, clearly belong to the sphere of the political; but others, such as authority, liberty, equality, and justice, have a wider application and are best considered as belonging to the sphere of the social in the sense of that term which includes the political. A more recent branch of philosophical inquiry, often called the methodology of the social sciences, is likewise part of social philosophy in this comprehensive sense. I do not propose to discuss any of its problems in this book, since its relation to the narrower subject of political philosophy is less close than is the philosophical treatment of the concepts of authority, liberty, equality, and justice. It is appropriate, however, to say something here about its relation to the traditional functions of philosophy.

The methodology of the social sciences is a branch of the philosophy of science. Many of the sciences have arisen out of philosophical questioning, and this is certainly true of the social sciences. Psychology originated both in epistemology (the theory of knowledge) and in moral philosophy; political science, economics, sociology, and social anthropology arose directly from moral, social, and political philosophy. This historical relation between the sciences and philosophy has led to the suggestion that science should be regarded as taking the place of philosophy.

The chief exponent of this view was Auguste Comte, often called the father of sociology. Comte[1] put forward a 'fundamental law of mental development', according to which all branches of human understanding go through three stages. In the first stage, the theological or fictive, men try to explain things by reference to supernatural forces. This becomes outmoded when philosophers question the validity of explanation by reference to mythical beings, and we then reach the second stage, the metaphysical or abstract, when explanation refers instead to reified abstractions, i.e. supposed real entities named by abstract terms such as 'absolute reality', 'absolute justice', or 'absolute motion' (Comte would say that Newtonian physics, which uses the concept of absolute motion, is not yet fully scientific). Once it is seen, however, that such terms are only abstractions from the language used to describe our experience of individual phenomena, and that there is no reason to suppose abstract terms to be the names of entities, we reach the third and final stage, the scientific or positive. (It should be noted that the transition from the metaphysical stage to the scientific, like the transition from the theological stage to the metaphysical, is similarly due to the critical work of philosophers, the chief architect of the later transition being David Hume.) In the third, positive or scientific, stage, explanation takes the form of showing correlations between the observed phenomena themselves; there is

[1] *Cours de Philosophie positive*, lecture 1.

no longer any attempt to go behind phenomena to hypothetical entities that cannot be observed. Comte called this kind of explanation 'positive' because it confines itself to positive or empirical fact, to what is known by observation to exist. (This use of the term 'positive' is obviously related to, though not quite the same as, the use noted earlier when the positive or factual was contrasted with the normative or ideal.) According to the positivist interpretation of science, the real point of Newton's theory of gravity is not to explain motion as caused by an unobservable force, but to relate together apparently different kinds of motion (e.g. that of the planets and that of a falling apple) by showing that they follow the same mathematical formula. In the field of social phenomena, explanation takes the form of showing how one species of social behaviour is correlated with another (e.g. style of life with occupation) or with factors in the environment (e.g. certain kinds of crime with poverty). There is no longer any point in explaining the rules of justice as being a reflection of absolute Justice, any more than as being the commands of supernatural beings. These supposed explanations either say nothing or else assume the existence of entities for which there is no evidence. Instead the rules of justice in a particular society are explained by showing how they fit in with some other social fact such as the survival of the group.

From this account of theology, metaphysics (or traditional philosophy), and science as successive modes of explanation, it follows that theology is outmoded by philosophy and that traditional philosophy in its turn is outmoded by science. Philosophy has been useful in its day, by helping scientific explanation to emerge; but once science has appeared, philosophy should disappear. Traces of this kind of view about the relation between philosophy and science may be seen in some later currents of thought. For example, the view that philosophy should confine itself to conceptual analysis and abandon critical evaluation may be regarded as a variant of the Comtean position. It says that the discovery of truth is a matter for science and not for philosophy; before the sciences were established, philosophers tried, in an amateurish way, to find out the facts; but now that the professionals are here, philosophy should leave the field to them. Philosophy still retains the task of examining the meaning of words, but according to some exponents of the view, this is only because there is not as yet, in their opinion, a sound science of language. Philosophical attention to the various dimensions of meaning will in time enable a proper science of language to arise, and then philosophy will really be out of a job or will have to think of a new one.

To the extent that theology and philosophy in the past did try to provide explanations of observable phenomena (as they undoubtedly did), their role in this regard has certainly been superseded by that of science. The development of the sciences, however, has itself provided philosophy with a new field of inquiry. The sciences are not static; they are developing all the time. And as a science or a group of sciences develops, it is apt to change its use of general concepts, sometimes without explicitly recognizing why or how the change has been made. This can lead to some confusion, at least in the minds of laymen, and at times perhaps in the minds of scientists themselves, between the new use of a concept and the old one which is still familiarly applied in ordinary life. The confusion, which in some instances depends on an apparent inconsistency, makes it necessary to clarify the concept. This is a philosophical task, though that is not to say that it is necessarily better undertaken by people called philosophers than by the scientists themselves. In place of prescientific philosophy, we now have the philosophy of science.

If a philosopher, as distinguished from a philosophically-minded scientist, is to be any good at the philosophy of science, he must not only be trained in logic and versed in conceptual analysis. He must know something of the concepts he is trying to clarify, and that means that he must have a fair knowledge of the relevant science or group of sciences. It is no use going in for a philosophical critique of the social sciences unless one has a reasonable acquaintance with two or three of them.

Although the philosophy of science requires specialized knowledge, it is not a new kind of philosophy but an application of the existing functions of philosophy to a new field. I have spoken so far of the clarification of changing concepts. In addition, the philosophy of science includes the critical evaluation of beliefs. I do not mean by this that the philosophy of science can or should try to usurp the function of science itself in testing the truth or falsity of scientific hypotheses. That would be absurd. What the philosophy of science subjects to critical evaluation are certain presuppositions that underlie the work of scientists. The need to do so arises in the way in which important philosophical problems usually arise. The development of a science is apt to produce apparent inconsistency, or lack of coherence, with beliefs of common sense or with the assumptions of another science or of some well-established special order of ideas which is not a theoretical or explanatory science. For example, is the general scientific assumption of causal necessity compatible with the assumption by common sense and by the well-established discipline of law that men are responsible for many of their actions? For that matter, do the biological sciences assume the same notion of causation as the physical sciences? Reflection on problems of this kind requires the kind of thing that I described in Section 2. The implications of the apparently inconsistent views need to be brought out, so as to show whether there really is or is not an inconsistency, and if there is, just at what point; then one or other or both of the conflicting views need to be revised so as to remove the inconsistency.

The very fact that the philosophy of science, or one part of it, is called methodology confirms that its business is not solely the clarification of concepts. The term 'methodology' means the study of method (though some people, rather foolishly, use it simply as a supposedly learned synonym for the word 'method' itself). Scientists, including social scientists, often use the term to mean the study of particular methods of research that are appropriate for particular kinds of investigation. Philosophers use the term in a broader sense to mean the study of methods of inquiry that are common to all the sciences, i.e. the kind of reasoning and testing that are commonly used. This is regarded as a philosophical problem because the idea that the main scientific method of reasoning was induction rather than deduction raised the philosophical question of how induction could be justified.

I myself think that the expression 'methodology of the social sciences' is too narrow to cover the philosophical questions that arise about the social sciences, and I prefer to speak of examining presuppositions and method. In the social sciences the number of presuppositions that are apt to produce difficulties is greater than in the natural sciences, and this for two reasons. First, the social sciences, as sciences, are relatively young disciplines and nothing like so well established as the natural sciences. They are still finding their feet and need the critique of philosophical questioning in a way that the natural sciences once did but do not now. Secondly, because the social sciences have human behaviour as their subject-matter, it is more difficult for them to keep consistently to positive facts and avoid implicit judgements of value. In addition to the problems raised by the assumption of causal laws, an assumption which the social sciences have derived from the natural sciences, there is a further set of problems concerning the question whether social studies can, or should try to, be 'value-free'. Even when an investigator thinks he is avoiding value-judgements, he may be unconsciously presupposing them in a way that affects his work; and this can be spotted by an outsider who is trained to look out for presuppositions.

The so-called methodology of the social sciences is approved of, as thoroughly respectable, by those philosophers who would say that the traditional aim of critically evaluating beliefs should be abandoned. They would also agree that 'methodology' in this connection includes the critique of presuppositions as well as of method proper. I have tried to show that the critique of presuppositions is simply a form of the critical evaluation of beliefs, so that in this new field at least the traditional aim of philosophy is agreed to be both practicable and desirable.

In fact, what is done by philosophy in the critical evaluation of beliefs is in principle the same as what is done in the clarification of concepts. The precise meaning, and the implications (including presuppositions), of a complex idea are analysed; its relations to other ideas are examined so as to draw attention to inconsistencies on the one hand and logical connections on the other; and, in order to remove the inconsistencies and produce a coherent synthesis, revision or improvement of one or more of the ideas is liable to be suggested.

The methodology of the social sciences is not part of political philosophy. It belongs to the wider subject of social philosophy. I have discussed it here in general terms in order to show that what is allowed on all hands to be a respectable function of philosophy is in fact an application of traditional functions. This, together with the analogy that can be drawn between critical evaluation and conceptual clarification, may help to remove the prejudice that critical evaluation is not philosophy.

II POLITICS AND THE STATE

1 THE SCOPE OF POLITICS

Modern writers on political science tend to distinguish between 'government' and 'politics'. 'Government' concerns the institutional framework of rule in a State, that is to say, the structure and procedure of the legislative body (in Britain, Parliament), of the executive and administrative bodies (roughly, the Cabinet, other holders of ministerial office, and the civil service), and of the analogous institutions in local government. 'Politics' concerns the behaviour of groups and individuals in matters that are likely to affect the course of government, e.g. in voting, in forming and running political parties, or in exerting influence in other ways on those responsible for the conduct of government. I shall be using the term 'politics' more widely so as to cover 'government' as well, and for this purpose I include under 'government' the institutions for interpreting and enforcing the law in addition to those for making and applying it.

How should one mark out the sphere of the political so as to distinguish it from the 'social', i.e. from all those activities in different forms of relationship between individuals which are not political? The old way of doing this is to say that the political is whatever concerns the State, and on the whole this way of delimiting the sphere of the political still seems to me the clearest. Of course we then need to say what is meant by the State, a question that I shall be discussing later in this chapter. It may be thought, however, that such an account of the political is too narrow. In the first place, it seems to cover only 'government' (including the procedures for interpretation and enforcement of law) but not the political behaviour of individuals and groups in voting, political parties, etc. Secondly, there are societies which are not States but which contain activities that we are bound to call political. Let us look at each of these objections in turn.

(1) The first objection is that, even in societies which are organized as States, not all political activity has to do with making, applying, interpreting, or enforcing the law. I think this objection is mistaken. When we vote in an election, we are deciding which persons shall form the legislature. When we join in the activities of a political party, or form a new one, we are seeking to give that party political power, and this means to give it the dominant voice in deciding what the law shall be. The policy of a political party is a set of proposals for organizing the affairs of the State, and that policy can be given effect only if it is adopted by the legislative and executive powers. Likewise, pressure groups or individuals who seek to influence Members of Parliament or Ministers or civil servants or public opinion are trying to cause their views to be given effect in legislation or in the application of the law. The whole process of political behaviour turns on the fact that there is the set of institutions called government for regulating the affairs of the society.

(2) The second objection is that there are societies which are not States but which nevertheless exhibit political activity. The objector may be thinking of primitive forms of society, such as tribal societies, who do not have the sophisticated political structure that we call the State. Such societies of course do have some pattern of regulation that is analogous to law and government in societies that are States. It is quite true that, strictly speaking, we cannot define the politics of such a society as that which concerns the State. The notion of a State has implications not only for the character of governmental regulation within the society but also for the relation of that society to others. As we shall see, the idea of a State in the modern world includes that of sovereignty, which concerns the relation of the State to other

States as well as its relation to groups and individuals who are part of it. Nevertheless a tribal society has a form of government, such as a chief or elders recognized as having the authority to lay down rules and to give decisions on disputed matters. So that, if we want to talk about the politics of such a society, we ought to speak of government (or, if that too suggests a more complex form of organization than is found, we may speak simply of rule) rather than of the State. Even in such societies, however, there is a system of law, at least in the form of customary rules or of authoritative decisions backed by power; and the politics of such a society, like the politics of a State, consists of the activities of making, applying, interpreting, and enforcing the system of law or rule, and the activities of influencing the former kind. For the purposes of political philosophy, the politics of such societies can largely be ignored, for the problems of political philosophy arise only in societies with a sophisticated set of ideas about their politics, and those societies usually have the form of organization that we call the State, though we do need to remember that not all the features of the modern State applied to the States of the past.

The objector may also be thinking, however, of a different type of instance. In ordinary parlance we may speak of 'politics' when talking about certain kinds of behaviour in a social unit that forms part of a larger society, organized as a State; and when we do talk, for example, of 'university politics' or 'church politics', we do not mean that the activities in question concern the larger society and its State organization. Members of a university or of a church may indeed campaign against some law that affects their activities, or against a policy that the Government of their State proposes to apply to them; and this is political behaviour of the usual kind. But within the university or the church there is much scope for the conduct of affairs as the smaller society itself may choose, and often of course there is difference of opinion among its members about the choices to be made. In such circumstances, some members take a leading part in influencing the decisions reached, while others do not. It may be said of one university teacher that he is active in 'university politics', and of another that he keeps out of 'university politics'. What is called 'politics' in this sort of context has to do with the framing of policies and the taking of decisions but not with the policies or decisions of the wider society of the State. It is called politics because, as in the political activities of the wider society, it concerns matters that are the subject of dispute.

I think that this use of the term 'politics' is metaphorical, parasitic on the normal use. Because political affairs include the seeking of power and the exercise of influence, the introduction of these features into other spheres of life is called 'politics'. Evidence of the metaphorical character of the expression can be found, I think, in the fact that the use of it is often as a term of abuse, suggesting that decisions on matters of university or church policy ought to be reached in a more 'rational' and 'objective' way, every member making up his mind on the issues as he sees them without being influenced behind the scenes, and everyone being content to count as one without seeking to dominate. Whether or not this ideal picture of rational, objective decisions is sensible, the pejorative use of the word 'politics' in such contexts implies that log-rolling and power-seeking are alien importations from politics proper, which is where they really belong. Although people are thereby led to speak of university or college or church politics, they would not find it natural to add that university or college or church politics is concerned with political matters.

People who are impressed by the objections that I have just considered are apt to define the sphere of the political either in terms of power or in terms of conflict. Politicians often say, naturally enough, that 'politics is about power' or that 'politics is the seeking and the exercise of power'. Such statements are quite clear when made in the speeches of practising politicians, and there is no reason to say that they mislead. But it is misleading to suggest that they can form a definition of politics in theoretical discussion. For we need to ask: with what kind of power is politics concerned? It is not mechanical power, such as the power of a steam engine. And if we confine ourselves to the powers of human beings, it is not their physical power, e.g. to run a mile or to twist literally one another's arms. Nor is it their will power, e.g. to try to stop smoking or to work an extra half-hour each day. We shall have to distinguish the kind of power we mean, by specifying it as political power; but of course it would be circular to define the political in terms of something else described as 'political'. If we then explain that the kind of human power we are talking about differs from physical power or will power in being the ability to get other people to do what one wants them to do, the definition becomes too wide, for this kind of power is exercised in many contexts other than the political. It can be seen not only in politics proper and in the so-called 'politics' of non-political societies such as a university or a church, but also in any effective exercise of authority. An army officer is usually able to get his subordinates to carry out his orders; so is a factory manager or a foreman. A parent is often (or should I say sometimes?) able to get his children to do what he says; so is a teacher with his pupils. Nor need we confine ourselves to instances where we may speak of authority. An armed bank-robber or a blackmailer is often able to make his victims hand over the cash. All these examples may be called instances of the exercise of power in the sense explained (though for some of them the use of the actual word 'power' seems odd, for reasons which will emerge when we discuss the ideas of power and authority in Chapter III, Section 4), but it would be absurd to say that they are examples of political power. Political power is indeed this kind of power, when exercised in a political context. If a politician says that politics is concerned with power, he means this kind of power, but he can take it for granted that we know he is referring to the seeking or exercise of it in a political context. What makes the context political cannot be explained by the idea of power.

The same goes for the alternative suggestion of defining the political in terms of conflict. There is political conflict, and there are also other kinds of conflict: armed conflict, which may or may not be connected with a political dispute; unarmed physical conflict, either in sport or in earnest; conflict of ideas, sometimes political, often not; and so on. Political conflict is usually not physical, though it may at times lead to physical conflict. It is a conflict of ideas as to what should be done when a decision needs to be taken for joint action, but such a conflict is political only if it occurs in a political context. I have heard one political scientist say that any conflict of the kind I have just described is political, irrespective of context; that in fact (the example was his, not mine), if two friends proposing to take an afternoon trip together on a tandem bicycle disagree as to whether they should go north or south, they are engaged in political conflict. This is absurd. We should similarly have to call political a disagreement between husband and wife whether they should spend a saved £50 on a washing-machine or a carpet, or between a group of children whether they should play tig or hop-scotch. If every disagreement between friends or associates about joint action is to be called a political conflict, the word 'political' is robbed of its distinctive meaning. Power and conflict are indeed key ideas for the understanding of political activity, but they cannot be used as defining terms in order to distinguish political from other social relationships.

I therefore prefer the old method of defining the scope of politics in terms of the State. The objections to it are not important for the purposes of political philosophy, and are in any case less strong than the objections to a definition in terms of power or of conflict, which in fact presupposes the older view. We must now consider the concept of the State itself, and in order to do so we must first distinguish two kinds of social groups.

2   ASSOCIATIONS AND COMMUNITIES

Ferdinand Tönnies drew a distinction between *Gemeinschaft* (community) and *Gesellschaft* (society or association). *Gemeinschaft* is the earlier form of social group; it involves an attitude of natural friendship and is not deliberately organized; it is based on 'natural will'. *Gesellschaft* comes at a later stage of development; it involves an attitude of deliberate planning or calculation; it is based on 'rational will'. To say that *Gesellschaft* occurs later does not imply that *Gemeinschaft* then ceases to exist; when we have come to make plans and form deliberate associations, we do not on that account cease to form friendships.

Tönnies' word *Gesellschaft* can be translated as 'society' or as 'association'. In ordinary English usage there is often little distinction between these two words. We may speak, for instance, of the Royal Society and the Law Society, but equally of the Association of University Teachers and the Political Studies Association. If I wanted to set up an organization to protect lecturers from catcalls, backchat, or paper missiles, I might call it indifferently a Society for the Prevention of Cruelty to Lecturers or a Lecturers' Protection Association. For the technical purposes of sociological theory, however, a good many sociologists nowadays use the word 'society' in a very broad sense for the whole of the subject-matter of sociology, and therefore tend to use the word 'association' alone for what Tönnies had in mind. I propose to follow their practice and to treat 'association' as a technical term with a sharply defined meaning. There is of course no suggestion that this is how the word is, or ought to be, used in ordinary life.

I define an association as a group of persons organized for the pursuit of a specified common purpose or set of common purposes. This definition lays down two conditions for applying the technical label of 'association' to a social group. First, the members of the group must have a specified common purpose or set of common purposes, and secondly, they must be organized for the pursuit of that purpose. I use the word 'purpose' rather than 'interest' because the latter term commonly means something that one wants or that will give satisfaction, while a purpose may in addition be the objective or aim of a rational decision to do something that is not necessarily dependent on wanting or on gaining satisfaction.

Not all social groups have a common purpose, and not all those that have a common purpose are organized for its pursuit. A number of people travelling together in a bus form a temporary group but not usually an association. They form a social group, in the sense in which that expression is used by sociologists, because their behaviour or disposition is liable to be affected to some extent by their awareness of each other. On entering or leaving the bus, for example, they will take care not to tread on the toes of other passengers; and if one of them happens to be the sort of person who does not care a hoot for other people's feelings and so treads firmly on all the toes in his path, he will at any rate be prepared for black looks and nasty remarks, so that his disposition, if not his actual behaviour, is affected by his awareness of the presence of others. But the group is not an association, because the passengers probably do not all have the same purpose; one is travelling in the bus in order to reach his place of work, another in order to see the beauties of the town. If they all happen to have the same destination, then to that extent their presence in the bus is due to a common purpose, but they have not made deliberate arrangements to travel together to achieve this purpose. If, as occasionally happens, they have in fact arranged that they should all travel together to a concert or for a day's outing, they form a temporary association.

We usually speak of associations when the group, deliberately organized for a common purpose, is not of such short duration. The organization, and the common purpose, usually last for some length of time. It need not be for very long. A group of tenants may form an association to try to get their rents reduced. If they should succeed after a month's campaigning, they may then disband the association, having achieved their purpose. On the other hand, the purpose of an association may be a continuing one. The members of an association for the prevention of cruelty to animals would like to think that the day will come when their association will no longer be needed, but they do not regard this as likely. A university, which has as its purposes the education of young people and the advancement of knowledge, can set no terminus on its pursuit of those purposes, since every new generation will need to be educated, and since the range of potential knowledge is presumably infinite.

In contrast to an association, a community does not have a specified set of purposes and need not be deliberately organized. Some examples are a family, a village, a nation. The Nation-*State* is highly organized for the pursuit of fairly definite pur-

poses, but we shall find reason to distinguish the nation from
the State. I have said that a community *need* not be deliberately
organized, and I am thereby qualifying Tönnies' distinction
between the two kinds of group in terms of 'natural will' and
'rational will'. A religious community may be ready to pursue
all sorts of common purposes and not just those few which some
people would label as specifically 'religious'; and certainly we
are inclined to call it a community rather than an association;
yet often it will exhibit deliberate organization. The same is true
of a communistic settlement such as an Israeli kibbutz. The close
ties produced by a shared life in such a group, and the common
possession of idealistic sentiments, are manifested in a loyalty
that Tönnies would call an expression of 'natural will'; but this
does not preclude the existence also of the 'rational will' of
organization.

3 PATTERNS OF REGULATION

Different patterns of regulation are to be found in organized
social groups. We are familiar with the terms 'democracy',
'monarchy', 'dictatorship', 'aristocracy', 'oligarchy', to describe
different patterns of political rule, depending on whether decisions are taken after general discussion and agreement, or by
the *fiat* of one person or a few in a position of authority. These
different forms of regulation, however, are not confined to the
State. Contrast the atmosphere of the Victorian family, or the
patria potestas of the Romans, with the way in which most
families are run in modern western society. Contrast the 'democratic' procedure of a religious community like the Quakers with
the hierarchical structure of the Roman Catholic Church, and
with the many gradations between these two extremes. Or
contrast the usual scheme of authority in a factory, where managers give orders and workers take them, with proposals for
consultation between managers and workers or, as it is sometimes
called, 'industrial democracy'. A school is usually conducted as
the headmaster and teachers decide, but occasionally a reformer
like Mr. A. S. Neill may experiment with the democratic method

of giving pupils an equal voice with masters in regulating discipline or even in deciding the curriculum.

These examples will make it plain that the democratic pattern of regulation, which most of us favour when we think of politics, is not necessarily the best one for organizing the affairs of every association or community. In a family, it is obvious that parents must be in a position of authority over young children because the latter are not yet able to decide wisely for themselves; and most of us would say this also about teachers and pupils in a school. It may be argued that the same is true of the other examples, even though most of the members of the group are adult. Some members are wiser than others for the purposes in hand; spiritual matters require wisdom; even political matters require educated judgement. On the other hand it may be argued that collective wisdom can be better than individual wisdom when the decision to be reached is not on a specialized matter requiring expertise; or that people resent having decisions taken for them by others, and prefer to make their own decisions and their own mistakes. Whichever set of arguments one prefers, they cannot be transferred without question from one type of association or community to all.

Aristotle[1] first drew attention to this matter when he classified different types of rule. He began with a familiar division of three types, rule by one man, by a few, and by all (or by the majority). But he then added that the question of who rules was less important than the aim of the ruler or rulers. Rule could be conducted for the common good of all or for the sectional good of the ruling party. The traditional classification needed to be duplicated, with one set of three 'right' or proper 'constitutions', in all of which the end pursued was the common good, and another set of three 'perverted' or improper 'constitutions', in which the end was restricted to the good of the ruler or rulers. Aristotle used the names 'royalty' and 'aristocracy' for 'right' rule by one man or a few, and the names 'tyranny' and 'oligarchy' for the 'perverted' forms. When it came to finding labels for the two

[1] *Nicomachean Ethics*, VIII. 10: *Eudemian Ethics*, VII. 9: *Politics*, I. 1, 7, 12; III. 6–8.

forms of majority rule, he tendentiously called the 'perverted' kind 'democracy' and used the names 'timocracy' and 'polity' for the 'right' kind. He thought that royalty and aristocracy were the best constitutions for a State, if one could be fortunate enough to secure these forms instead of their perversions. But he added that a different choice should be made in deciding the best forms of rule in a family; royalty was right for the relation of a father to his children, 'polity' (in his ethical works Aristotle said aristocracy) for the relation between husband and wife, and tyranny (or despotism) for the relation between the head of the family and its slaves. Needless to say, he gave reasons for his view that in the last example it was proper (and not, as in the State, a perversion) for the master to seek his own interest only in his rule over his slaves. We shall not expect to agree with Aristotle's arguments for this position or for the view that it is 'natural' or proper for anyone to be a slave. The point of interest for our present discussion is that Aristotle realized that the kind of organization that is best for a State may not be the best for a different type of association or community.

A further point worth noting in Aristotle's discussion is this. Since the 'perverted' forms of rule aim only at the interest of the ruler or rulers, oligarchy and 'democracy', he says, are examples of rule in the interests of particular classes, namely the rich and the poor respectively. It so happens, Aristotle adds, that the rich are always a minority and the poor a majority; but if one were to find a State in which there were more rich men than poor, then rule by the rich in their own interests would be essentially the same as oligarchy (even though, strictly speaking, the word 'oligarchy' means rule by the few), and rule by the poor in their own interests would be essentially the same as what Aristotle calls democracy (even though, strictly speaking, the word 'democracy' means rule by all or most of the people). The character of a constitution is bestowed on it, in Aristotle's opinion, less by the number of the rulers than by their aim. This means that the traditional first classification in terms of the number of rulers has been completely replaced, in Aristotle's final view, by his second classification in terms of the purpose of the ruler or rulers and, where there is more than one ruler, in terms of the social character of the ruling class. Since the essence of oligarchy is not rule by a few but rule in the interests of the wealthy, it would be better to call it plutocracy; and since the essence of democracy, as Aristotle understands it, is rule in the interests of the poor, one might suggest, though he himself does not, coining a new name for it, 'penetocracy' (from *penes*, the Greek word for 'poor').

Aristotle did not think that *all* rule is carried on in the interest of the ruling class or ruling group. He believed that it was possible to find 'constitutions' or forms of rule in which the rulers pursued the interest of the whole society. He acknowledged that we were unlikely to find political associations in which the ideal forms of royalty and aristocracy would be realized, and so he was ready to settle for 'polity' as the best that could be secured in practice. But this is true only of the State. In a family it is perfectly possible for a father to rule 'royally', i.e. taking the decisions alone but in the interests of the family as a whole. One often hears it said that in Marxist theory (I am not competent to express an opinion whether this was the view of Marx himself) *all* rule is class-rule, conducted only in the interests of the ruling group. It is presupposed that self-interest is the sole motive of action, and that a member of a ruling group will join in seeking the interest of the group because that is the best way to secure his own interest. The thesis has a certain plausibility and appearance of hard-headed realism when we are asked to look at the actual conduct of political parties, whether in power or out of it, or at the behaviour of bosses and workers in a factory. One may doubt whether it is always true of a factory, though it often is and though it was generally taken for granted in the nineteenth century with its concept of economic man (hence perhaps the Marxist generalization). But it is certainly not true of most families or religious communities or schools. (If Mr. Squeers were a typical schoolmaster, Dickens's portrayal of him would have lost its point.) A comparison between the State and other organized groups, such as Aristotle initiated with his comparison and contrast between State and family, can show us that the psychological presupposition of the class-theory of rule is unsound. A concern for the general good is less likely to show itself in a large association than in a small one, such as a school, or than in a community such as a family or a church. Self-interest and class-interest do count for a lot in politics. But this cannot be because self-interest is the sole motive of action. Those who have a position of power in a family, a church, or a school, rarely exercise it in the interests of themselves alone.

4   STATE AND NATION

It seems best to regard the State as an association rather than a community. The State is certainly organized, indeed the most highly organized of all forms of association. It is not easy, however, to specify a definite, limited set of purposes that may be attributed to it. The Greek city-state had a virtually unlimited set of social functions; those of the modern State have been much extended in the course of the nineteen and twentieth centuries. In a famous passage near the beginning of his *Politics* (I. 2), Aristotle says that the *polis* comes into being for the sake of life, but that once it exists it has as its purpose the good life. It is customary to translate '*polis*' as 'the State'; and so some philosophers, influenced by Aristotle, have said that the purpose of the State is the good life, the good life as a whole, all purposes that men think worth pursuing. But the Greek *polis* was more of a community than the modern State. 'The good life', that is to say, the sum of all approved common purposes, may be regarded as the function of community. The Greek city-state, so called, was not a State in the modern sense, which leaves much of 'the good life' to other social agencies and to individuals.

One might argue that the whole of the life of a community *should* be organized by the State, that the State should identify itself with the community whose membership it shares, as was true of the Greek city-state, where religion, morals, and art, as well as order and defence, were all part of the business of the *polis*. On the other side, one may argue that it is impossible in a large community, or that it is undesirable in any community, to organize all social purposes centrally and to leave no scope for private initiative. But at any rate the fact is that the modern State, except for the totalitarian State, does not even try to take upon itself the organization of all communal purposes, so that its purposes are in practice limited.

The State in the modern world is usually a Nation-State, i.e. a nation organized as an association. The nation is a community, a group with all the conditions for a common life and giving rise to natural sentiments of loyalty and identification, but not limited to a specific set of purposes. In order to see the difference, consider two senses in which the word 'nationality' is used. The Visitors' Book at a hotel usually has a column headed 'Nationality'. Some Scotsmen tend to write 'Scots' or 'Scottish' in this column, others 'British'. In the legal sense of the term, which is what the Visitors' Book is after, they all have British nationality. This legal concept may also be called citizenship. In the relevant legal language of the U.S.A., one speaks of a 'citizen' of the United States (because an expression parallel to 'British subject' would be inappropriate for people who do not owe allegiance to a King or Queen). In the Commonwealth we speak of British nationality and, in addition, of citizenship either of the United Kingdom and Colonies, or of a particular Dominion. A Scot, like an Englishman, has a British passport. The law does not recognize any such thing as Scottish nationality. Apart from the legal concept, however, there is also what has been called the concept of 'personal nationality'. This consists in a feeling of 'belonging' to a group which inhabits (or, as with Scots Canadians, once inhabited) a common territory, shares a common language and common traditions, has the memory of a common history, and looks forward to a common future. In this sense of nationality, a man may think of himself as having Scottish or English or Welsh nationality. A 'nationalist', e.g. a Scottish nationalist, is one who feels personal nationality strongly and who urges that his nation be organized as a separate State.

As my example shows, nation and State do not always coincide. Some nations are divided into, or distributed among, more than one State; some States comprise more than one nation. The United

Kingdom includes most members of the English nation, the Scottish nation, the Welsh nation, and—well, I do not know whether one should call the people of Ulster a separate nation or part of the Irish nation. The concept of a nation is imprecise. The people of Ulster share with their southern neighbours affection for the landscape, way of life, and perhaps even the weather, of Ireland, but a history of religious and political conflict divides them in sentiment, just as the border divides them in legal status. A nation can be formed into a State, but equally a State can give rise to a nation. Should we say that the people of the United Kingdom form a nation in a looser sense than that in which England and Scotland are nations? At any rate they form a community, made so, in part, by the political organization, and the consequent economic organization, that link together the three nations inhabiting Great Britain and the fourth nation, or part of a nation, inhabiting Northern Ireland.

Even when the nation and the State have the same territorial boundaries, membership of the two is not necessarily identical. An immigrant who becomes naturalized and so a citizen of the State, with all the rights and obligations of the natural-born citizen, will not, for some time at least, feel himself to be a member of the nation and may not be accepted as such by others. In general, nations and States in the modern world tend to coincide in membership, if only because nationalism gives rise to new Nation-States and the ties of statehood give rise to the feeling of being a nation. Yet the difference in character between nation and State remains. The nation is a community, the State an association; membership of the nation is a matter of sentiment, depending on common experience and history, while membership of the State is a matter of legal status.

5 DISTINCTIVE FEATURES OF THE STATE

If we want to define the concept of the State, we must differentiate the State from other species of the same genus. The State is an association, but how does it differ from other associations? Let us consider some suggestions.

(a) Universal jurisdiction within territorial boundaries

We have already seen that, even where nation and State have the same territorial boundaries, membership of the two is not absolutely identical. A person may be a member of the State but not of the nation; and conversely. Membership of the State applies to nearly everyone who lives within its boundaries. I say 'nearly' everyone, because the rights and privileges of a citizen are not automatically and at once granted to everyone who comes to live within the boundaries of the State. Many States accord citizenship to anyone born within their territory, but a foreigner who immigrates and wants to become a citizen has to wait for a time and to show that he is worthy of citizenship by naturalization. Citizenship, or membership of the State, carries obligations as well as rights and privileges. Certain of the obligations imposed and of the rights protected by the State, however, apply to all persons who happen to be within its boundaries, whether permanently or temporarily, irrespective of whether they are citizens. For example, a foreign resident does not have the right to vote, and if he is a temporary visitor he may not be obliged to pay some of the taxes levied on citizens and on foreigners domiciled in the country; but he is obliged to obey the ordinary laws of the land, and can be punished if he does not. (There is the exceptional case of diplomatic immunity, which is granted by mutual agreement between States and for the sake of mutual convenience; but this need not concern us here.) Conversely he is equally entitled to protection of common rights under the criminal and civil law of the land. Just as he will be liable to punishment for stealing from a citizen or anyone else, so a citizen or anyone else will be liable to punishment for stealing from him. The jurisdiction of the State is applied universally to all persons who happen to be within its bounds.

The bounds of jurisdiction are limited, roughly to the recognized territory of the State (with some extension to territorial waters, air space, and ships flying the State's flag in international waters). These bounds are defined by the general agreement of States in international law, designed to mitigate potential sources of conflict. States divide the population of the world between them, and each exercises universal jurisdiction within its boundaries. This is true of no other form of association. I do not mean that it is impossible in principle for any other type of association, e.g. a Church, to possess the feature of exercising universal jurisdiction within a territory, but only that this feature is in fact confined to States in the world of to-day.

(b) Compulsory jurisdiction

The second feature of the State to be considered is closely linked with the first. The universal jurisdiction of a State within a territory means that everyone in that territory is subject to its rules. A universal statement is often equivalent to a statement of necessity, and it is so in this instance: anyone within the borders of a State *must* be subject to its rules, whether he likes it or not.

A universal statement is not always equivalent to a statement of necessity. Sometimes 'All *A*s are *B*s' does not imply 'Anything that is an *A* must be a *B*'. There may be a society in which everyone is, as a matter of fact, a member of a particular Church, as perhaps was once true of the inhabitants of Utah. It would not necessarily follow that one could not be a member of that society without belonging to that particular Church. The inhabitants may all have chosen to be members of the Church; or at least, it may be that none have chosen not to be members of the Church although they could opt out if they wanted to do so. With the jurisdiction of the State, however, there is no choice about it. If you reside in, or even visit, a certain territory, you are willy-nilly subject to the jurisdiction of the State which controls it. You cannot say that you choose not to be subject to its laws. If you are in the country, you are necessarily bound by its laws, and if you disobey any of them you will be liable to punishment on the assumption that you are bound by them.

Compulsory subjection to the jurisdiction of a State is of course dependent on the condition of remaining within the State's boundaries. Once upon a time, if a group of people preferred not to be subject to the laws of their State, they could leave it and found a new community elsewhere with rules of their own choosing. To-day it is still possible, for some people, to emigrate from a country if they do not like its laws. But it is not possible for them to set up an entirely new community with its own laws. All inhabitable parts of the earth (and nearly all the uninhabitable parts too) have been commandeered by now and organized into new States or brought under the jurisdiction of existing States. If you do not like the laws of Britain, and if you can afford to emigrate, you can escape the jurisdiction of the United Kingdom but not the jurisdiction of any State. If you emigrate to Australia, you are at once subject to the jurisdiction of that State. This apart from the fact that many people who would like to leave their State do not have the money to do so, or, in some countries, require and cannot obtain an exit visa, or cannot acquire permission to enter or to reside permanently in the country of their choice.

The first feature of the State that we considered, universal jurisdiction, is now true of no other type of association and can therefore serve as a distinctive characteristic differentiating the modern State from other associations. Does this apply also to the second feature? It is often said that the State is distinctive in being a compulsory association while all others are voluntary.

If we may, for the moment, consider communities along with associations, it is not in fact true that joining any other society than the State is a matter of choice. One is born a member of a family, and sometimes of a religion. Nor can one choose to leave a family, in the sense of renouncing biological kinship. But one can choose to leave a family considered as a social group; that is to say, one can choose to renounce consorting with the other members or acknowledging any obligations towards them. Presumably the same is true of religious communities. There may be some religious communities which say that if one is born into them one remains a member despite apostasy or deliberate flouting of their rules and practices; but since they cannot give effect to this doctrine of continued bonds of allegiance, as the State can, the recalcitrant may treat it as myth.

Some people are more or less compelled to join a Trade Union if they wish to follow a particular occupation. They can choose to leave, but only at some sacrifice, by abandoning that occupation for another one. This is not unlike the possibility of escaping the trammels of a particular State at the cost of emigrating to another. Similarly, in some districts a failure to act as a member of the church or chapel may involve sacrifice of a kind, such as facing social and perhaps economic ostracism. The compulsion to conform which is exercised by the State is greater in degree than that exercised by some other social groups, including associations like Trade Unions, but it does not appear to be different in kind so far as its compulsory character is concerned.

(c) Functions

Different associations have different functions. I have already noted, in Section 4, the view that the State should undertake all communal purposes. Some philosophers have accordingly held that the State differs from other associations in that it is omni-competent in its functions; indeed that it includes all other associations, being an association of associations, the whole community organized in all its aspects as a comprehensive association. This view has been influenced by undue concentration on the theory and practice of ancient Greece, where the city-state really was the whole community organized, and where Plato and Aristotle, in consequence, regarded the *polis* as omni-competent. Some later philosophers have followed them and have considered the more limited functions of the modern State to be a defect, neglecting the difference that is made by the size of the two kinds of State and by the different character of religion among the Greeks and in the modern world. A further influence has been the analogy between the State and an organism, again owing much to Greek theory and especially to Aristotle.

To say that the State is omnicompetent may mean either of three things: that the State may, or that it does, or that it should, undertake any and every possible function. We shall consider in a later chapter (V, Section 3) the views that it may or that it should. In practice, no State does. What are called totalitarian States may claim to do so, but they do not altogether succeed, e.g. in regard to religion. It is worth noting that the claim to identify the State completely with the community tends to go along with making religion, or a substitute for religion, a part of politics. This was true of ancient Greece, and it is true of communist ideology to-day; communism may be regarded as a kind of religion as well as a political system.

What, then, are the functions, in practice, of the modern State? Its primary function is to settle and prevent conflict, or to put it in another way, the keeping of order and the maintenance of security. Two kinds of security are involved, security within the community and security against injury from external sources. Security within the community means security against deliberate infringement of rights in respect of person or property (e.g. against assault or theft), and against non-deliberate damage (e.g. owing to negligence). Security against external injury likewise covers both deliberate harm (as in acts of war by other States) and non-deliberate damage (as when a home industry suffers from the dumping of excessively cheap foreign goods). Internal security is maintained by the keeping of order, that is to say, the inculcation of regular modes of behaviour that will guarantee such security. The criminal law, and much of the civil law, of a State are designed to produce this. It is often said therefore that the primary purpose of the State is to preserve 'law and order', but strictly speaking this confuses purpose and method. The preservation of order is the aim or purpose; law, with its sanctions, is the main method used by the State to give effect to this and some of its other purposes. Security against external injury is pursued by the maintenance of armed forces, the making of treaties and alliances with foreign States, and economic measures such as trade agreements and tariffs.

The primary function of the State that I have just described may be called a negative function, in the sense that it is the prevention of harm to existing rights or existing well-being, as contrasted with a positive function of adding to well-being or of adding new rights or redistributing old ones. The aim of the negative function is to preserve the *status quo* of rights and opportunities. In the seventeenth and eighteenth centuries, liberal democratic theory held that this was the sole function

of the State. The promotion or pursuit of further positive good
was thought to be the business of the individual. He should be
left with as much liberty as possible for that end. State action,
which takes the form of laying down and enforcing laws, restricts liberty, in that its requirement to do or not to do this or
that limits our freedom to do as we please. The purpose of such
laws, it was said, was to prevent individuals from encroaching on
each other's rights or liberties. The business of the State was to leave
to each individual as large an area of liberty as possible. Its inter-
ventions should therefore be minimal, limited to the negative
function of preventing one individual or group from encroaching
on the liberty of another. As for the pursuit of positive good—
happiness, culture, moral improvement—that was a matter for the
individual himself. He was free to promote his good if he chose
and if he had the ability. If he failed, whether through lack
of effort or lack of ability or sheer misfortune, that was a pity,
but it did not call for remedies by the State. A voluntary association, such as a charitable organization, might do something
about it; but not the State. The State should keep out of such
matters. Its laws might be said to echo the sentiment satirized
by Arthur Hugh Clough:

> Thou shalt not kill, but need'st not strive
> Officiously to keep alive.

This doctrine of the minimal State is at the opposite extreme
from the doctrine that the State should undertake all possible
social functions. As I have said, the minimal view was popular
in the seventeenth and eighteenth centuries. Nowadays almost
all States add a positive function to the negative one of protecting established rights. There is a considerable difference
between liberal democracies and communist States in the extent
to which they pursue the positive function. And among the
liberal democracies themselves, some have moved farther than
others from the idea of the minimal State. The U.S.A., for
example, has moved less far than Britain. Even in the U.S.A.,
however, the State does not confine itself to the negative function
of preserving order and security.

The newer, positive function of the modern State may be described as the promotion of welfare and justice. It is now regarded as a responsibility of the national community as a whole, in its organized capacity, to increase in some degree the well-being of its members and to make more fair the distribution of rights which they enjoy. Since the notion of justice is used to cover anything that has to do with rights, one may say that the minimal State too has justice as its aim. Its practice of justice, however, is a conserving (one can even say conservative) function, while the positive function is one of reforming the order of legal rights so as to accord more closely with current moral ideas of justice (often called 'social justice').

'Welfare' is a vague term. It may refer only to means to physical well-being, such as food, houses, and medical care. Or it may include also some means to mental or spiritual well-being, such as education, art galleries, museums, and theatres. It would be generally agreed nowadays that a State should be responsible for seeing that some measure of material well-being is available for all its members, that, for example, no-one should be left to starve by reason of unemployment or sickness. But there is not general agreement about the extent to which this should go. In Britain we have a National Health Service, but many people in the United States are opposed to the idea of 'socialized medicine'. The modern notion of the 'Welfare State' in many countries of Western Europe and the Commonwealth is that the State should be responsible for providing a basic minimum of material welfare for all, and that the individual should himself be responsible for trying to rise above that basic minimum; but there is difference of opinion between different political parties and other groups on where the line of the basic minimum should be drawn. When it comes to non-material well-being, there is even less agreement about the role of the State. Communist States include a great deal. All States make some provision for education, but in liberal democratic countries it is generally thought that education should not be a monopoly of the State. Once we go beyond education, and facilities such as museums and art galleries which among other things contribute to education, we are on delicate

ground. In Britain, most of us would think that the State should
be very little concerned with aesthetic enjoyment (to say nothing
of religious activities), though in fact a certain amount of
financial support is given by the State nowadays not only to art
galleries but also to drama, music, opera, ballet, and even, in a
small way, to the writing of literature. But apart from education,
these things would not be regarded, outside communist countries,
as essential responsibilities of the State.

Do the functions of the State serve to differentiate it from
other associations? The negative function does, when taken as a
whole, but the positive does not. Part of the negative function
can be a function of other associations too. An organization like
Securicor, which offers to guard money or other valuables in
transit, has security as its function, though only in a limited
field of activity. An association of a different kind, a school or a
university for example, may have a disciplinary procedure to
keep good order, but this is subordinate to the actual purpose of
the association and is in any case restricted to order within the
association. Only the State has as its actual purpose internal
order within the association, and only the State deals both with
internal order and with security from external injury.

The positive function, however, is not exclusive to the State.
Many associations and communities seek to promote the welfare
and just treatment of their members; this is true of the family,
religious communities, charitable organizations, Trade Unions,
and similar occupational associations. In fact the Welfare State
has simply taken over a part of a social function that was formerly
left entirely, and is still left to a considerable extent, to voluntary
effort by charitable organizations and individuals. The difference
is that when responsibility to aid the poor and the weak is taken
over by the State, it is no longer a voluntary matter but is made
compulsory by law. This leads us to the next distinctive feature
of the State, the methods whereby its functions are carried out.

(d) Methods

The main method whereby the State carries out its functions is
the system of law, that is, rules backed by coercive power. This

method plays relatively little part, however, in the pursuit of security from external injury. There coercive power alone, in the shape of the armed services, and agreements with other States that may not have the force of law, are more prominent. But even in this field law has some place, both the rules of international law and such domestic laws as relate to the raising and maintenance of the armed services or to the imposition of tariffs and quotas. To preserve internal security, and to fulfil the positive function of promoting welfare and justice, the State relies almost entirely on the method of law.

All three 'powers' of the State, legislative, executive, and judicial, are concerned in the employment of this method. The Legislature makes the law, or more properly, makes part of it, namely statutes. The Executive (which in this context may be taken to comprise not only the Government but also the vast host of public servants, i.e. the civil service, the police and prison services, and the armed services) gives effect to the law by applying and enforcing it. The Judiciary interprets the law and also, in fact though not in formal theory, helps to make law in the field of common or case law. So central and pervasive is law to the concept of the State that one theorist, Hans Kelsen, has held that the State is best understood as simply being the system of law.

How does law distinguish the State from other associations? All, or nearly all, associations regulate the conduct of their members by a system of rules, and often these are set out formally in a constitution. The difference between the rules laid down by the State, which we call laws, and the rules of other associations lies in a combination of two things.

First, the rules of the State are backed by force. The decisions of the courts are backed by the power of the police and prison services, and in the last resort the Executive can, if need be, use the power of the armed forces. It should be noted that the difference does not lie simply in sanctions, i.e. in penalties for the breach of rules, but in the power to enforce the sanctions. Any association may impose penalties for the infringement of its rules by a member. A Trade Union, the headmaster and other teachers in a school, a body like the General Medical Council that regulates the conduct of a profession, may all prescribe penalties (such as fines, deprivations of various kinds, suspension, or expulsion) for the breach of rules. In some of them, the school for instance, the penalties can be enforced to a certain extent, but only to a certain extent. If the erring member of the association refuses to accept the penalty, or, in the case of the child at school, can get some responsible adult to question the propriety of enforcing it, the association must appeal to the authority of the State's laws, from which its own authority is derived, and if necessary the disciplinary decision of the association can be tested before a court, whose judgement is susceptible of enforcement by State power.

The mere use of coercive power is, of course, no monopoly of the State. Armed robbers and bullies use it too. I have been speaking of the place of coercive power in enforcing the *rules* of an association, not just in enforcing the will of an individual or body of men. Occasionally, however, the latter can turn into the former, as when an unlawful gang like the Mafia in Sicily virtually acts as if it were exercising the functions of a State. To bring out fully the difference between the rules of the State and those of other associations, we must add a second feature of State law. This has already been mentioned by implication in what I have said about the authority of State law in relation to that of other rules. The rules of other associations within the jurisdiction of a State, and the authority which those associations possess to make and apply their rules, are subordinate to the rules of the State. The State's rules are the supreme rules. This is what is meant by State sovereignty, a concept so important for the ideas associated with the modern State that it needs to be listed separately.

(e) Sovereignty

To say that the State is sovereign is to say that the State has supreme or final authority in a community, that its rules override the rules of any other association. Other associations within the State's territory, e.g. a borough, a factory, a Trade Union, a university, are subject to the authority of the State. Such legal powers as they have are granted to them by the legal authority of the State. They may make rules only to the extent that the laws of the State permit or require them to do so. Any internal dispute within such an association (e.g. between a member and the presiding body), or any dispute between one such association and another (e.g. between a borough and a university), is subject to jurisdiction by the State's courts. But the legal powers of the State itself are not subject to any higher authority—in the world as now constituted.

In earlier times the authority of a King could be held to be subject to the higher authority of a universal Church; and one can imagine that at some future time the authority of States may be subject to the higher authority of an international organization, just as now the authority of a non-sovereign state like Alabama or Michigan, which is a constituent member of a federal union, is in many fields of action subordinate to the authority of the federal State. That is why people talk of 'giving up our sovereignty' when there is discussion about membership of a supra-national political organization such as a United States of Europe (or, for that matter, the European Common Market when the political provisions of the Treaty of Rome are given full effect), or such as a revised form of the United Nations Organization. But at present the sovereign State is a final authority.

You may ask: what about international law? Is not that superior in authority to the law of an individual State, and is not the International Court of Justice at the Hague, or the European Court of Human Rights at Strasbourg, superior to the courts of England or Scotland? The answer to the first part of this question is not altogether clear, since international law does serve to define the bounds of jurisdiction of sovereign States, and in other respects the authority of international law is developing markedly in our own time. Nevertheless, the short general answer to the question is 'No', from a legal point of view. From a moral point of view, the answer may be 'Yes'. That is to say, we may think that international law *ought* to count as superior to municipal (i.e. national) law. But the present legal position is that many (though not all) rules of international law are legally binding on a State only if that State voluntarily accepts them as binding; and if it does, a method frequently used is to incorporate the relevant part of international law within its own municipal law. The relation of an international court to the English courts is not that of a court of appeal to a court of first instance. Some day it may be, and the beginnings of a move in that direction may be seen in the authority of the European Court of Human Rights to give a decision on a complaint brought by an individual against his own State after he has exhausted all the remedies available to him in the courts of that State.

Of course the law of the State is not held to be superordinate over international law or over the law of another State. To say that the law of the State has supreme authority is not to say that it has no equals, that it is the *only* final legal authority in the world. States recognize the equal sovereignty of other States, and they also recognize that international law has its own independent form of authority. To say that the State has sovereign or supreme authority is to say that its legal authority is not subordinate to any other authority, while at the same time it is superordinate over the authority of other associations which carry on their affairs within the territorial boundaries of its jurisdiction.

This survey of suggested distinctive features of the State has shown that the State is differentiated from other associations by its universal jurisdiction, its negative function, and the special character of law in being backed by force and having sovereign authority. The compulsory nature of State jurisdiction, and the State's positive function, differ in degree but not in kind from similar features of some other associations. We may therefore define the State as an association designed primarily to maintain order and security, exercising universal jurisdiction within territorial boundaries, by means of law backed by force and recognized as having sovereign authority.

III SOVEREIGNTY, POWER, AND AUTHORITY

1 STATE SOVEREIGNTY

In the modern world we speak of 'sovereign States'. Not all states are sovereign States. Those that are constituent members of a federal commonwealth or union do not possess sovereignty, since they are subject, except in certain limited fields of action, to the sovereignty of the federal State or union. The sovereignty which is attributed to States that are not constituent members of a federal sovereign State, is particularly important in regard to international relations. State sovereignty has not always been a feature of international society in the past, and it may not always be so in the future. For three or four centuries, however, State sovereignty has been an essential factor of politics, and that position is likely to remain for some time to come. It is therefore of some importance to be clear what the concept means and what it does not mean.

A much disputed question in political science is where the sovereignty of a State is located. Does it reside in a legislature which is empowered to make statutes that can override rules of common law or repeal earlier statutes? Or in a supreme court that can determine whether an Act of the legislature is constitutional? Or does it reside in the constitution itself, or in the body that is empowered to amend the constitution? Hence we hear of 'the sovereignty of Parliament' or sometimes of 'the sovereign people'. I shall not be concerned with this tricky question, but with the meaning of 'sovereignty' when applied to the State as a whole. The activities of the State are divided among different bodies, none of which may be supreme in all respects. In relation to other associations, however, and to other States, the State as a whole is regarded as sovereign.

Sovereignty means supremacy. But supremacy of what? In the preceding chapter I have defined sovereignty in terms of legal authority. To say that the State is sovereign is to say that its rules, the laws, have final authority; there is no appeal from them to any more ultimate set of rules, while the rules made by other associations or communities are subordinate to the authority of the State's rules. A number of theorists would say that although this concept of legal sovereignty is doubtless of use to lawyers, it has little relevance to politics, for which we need a different concept, that of political sovereignty, to be defined in terms of power instead of legal authority. I think that the so-called concept of political sovereignty, defined in terms of power, is simply a confusion. Power is undoubtedly essential for politics, and for law too, but I do not think that State sovereignty can be understood as anything other than legal sovereignty.

2 THE POWER THEORY

Let me put the case for a power theory of sovereignty by considering why the legal concept may be supposed defective for the purposes of politics. Legal sovereignty treats the State, or the State's system of law, as a final legal authority. The concept is to be understood from a legal point of view. From a *moral* point of view, one may say that the laws of the State do not have final authority. If an individual's conscience tells him that he ought not to obey some particular law, then, from a moral point of view, he is entitled to disobey, for in most matters of morals (some would say, in all matters of morals) the final authority is conscience. But he is not legally entitled to disobey. If he were, then the law which is in question would not have ultimate legal authority; to say that he is legally entitled to disobey is to imply that there is a superior *law* which permits disobedience to the particular law.

We can illustrate the difference by the example of conscientious objection to military service. When there is conscription, a law makes all fit men of certain ages, and perhaps women too, liable to be called up for military service. If an individual has a properly conscientious objection to military service, he is morally entitled to refuse to perform it. Is he also legally entitled to refuse? That depends on the law of the country concerned. If, as is the case in some countries, the law makes no provision for conscientious objection, he is not legally entitled to refuse to serve; but it is a matter of conscience, i.e. of moral judgement, for him to decide what, morally, he ought to do, taking account of the fact that there is, in general, a moral obligation to obey the law, though this obligation may on occasion conflict with some other moral obligation. If the individual decides that his moral duty is to disobey the law, the State is still legally entitled to subject him to the penalties prescribed for breaking this law; and in some circumstances the individual may even consider that he is morally as well as legally obliged to accept the prescribed penalties. In Britain, however, when we have conscription, it is accompanied by legal provision for conscientious objection. Our conscription law has said that all fit men of certain ages are liable to be called up for military service *unless* (among other exceptions) they establish to the satisfaction of a tribunal that they have a conscientious objection. An individual is therefore legally, as well as morally, entitled to refuse to serve because of a conscientious objection. But the legal provision covers only such conscientious objection as is recognized by a tribunal. If an individual fails to satisfy a tribunal that he has a conscientious objection, he is legally obliged to obey a calling-up notice, but he himself may decide that he is morally obliged to refuse, in which case he is legally liable to the penalties prescribed by the State.

It will be seen, then, that the assignment of final authority is made from a certain point of view. It may be the legal point of view or it may be the moral point of view. Now the idea of State sovereignty as I have previously described it, the idea that the laws of the State are a final authority, is taken from the legal point of view, and this means from the point of view of the

State itself, since the law simply is the set of rules whereby the State conducts its affairs. Clearly it is possible for a different association or community to hold similarly that, from its own point of view, it is the final authority. Just as an individual may say that, from the moral point of view, his own conscience is the final authority, so a Church may say that, from the religious point of view, its own rules are the final authority. Furthermore, a Church may also say that there is no aspect of life that falls outside the scope of religion. Consequently it is possible for a Church to maintain that political decisions are subordinate to religious judgement, and that the rules of the Church are more authoritative than those of the State.

This is what was claimed by the Pope in the Middle Ages. The conflict between Pope and Emperor was one in which each side claimed to be the superior authority. At that time there would not have been general agreement that States were sovereign, i.e. supreme authorities. When all the Kings of Christendom acknowledged obedience to the Pope, their own authority was not supreme; it was a subordinate authority. But when the medieval structure of society broke down, there was a need for recognition of a new form of supreme authority, and each State claimed such authority for itself; that is to say, it claimed to be its own master and subject to no dictation by any higher authority. Thus the doctrine of State sovereignty arose together with the rise of separate national States, owing to the breakdown of the universal organized community of Christendom.

In the conflict between Church and State, each side claimed authority, but in practice the State won out because of its superior power. It should be noted that 'power' in this connection means not simply the ability to have one's will carried out, but the ability to do so by the threat of force. The superior power of the State was the power of force of arms. Consequently some people would say that the only concept of State sovereignty that really counts is a matter of power in this sense, and not a matter of authority. Any association or community may claim to be a final authority from its own point of view, and any individual may claim the same for his own judgement of what he ought to do. The thing that really counts, however, it would be said, is the power to enforce such a claim. The individual may claim that he is entitled to disobey the law, but the State has the power to force him to comply with its requirements. I said earlier that a conscientious objector who has not been able to satisfy the State authorities may think himself morally entitled or obliged to disobey the law, and also morally obliged to accept the legal penalties. He will take the latter view if he acknowledges that he has a general moral obligation to conform to the State's requirements even though he thinks that this general obligation is overridden, in regard to the performance of military service, by the obligation not to take human life. But of course an individual's conscientious objection may be wider than that, and he may consider that he has no moral obligation to accept the legal penalties. In that event, if he is imprisoned, the penalty is forcibly imposed on him. Similarly a Church may consider that the State does not have the right to restrict its activities; but the State has power, while the Church has not; and so the Church, it may be said, is forced into subjection to the State.

It is for such reasons as these that some theorists speak of a concept of 'political sovereignty' distinct from legal sovereignty. The argument is designed to show that the sovereignty of the State should be defined, for the purposes of politics, as supremacy of coercive power rather than of legal authority. Does the argument succeed in showing this? That the possession of coercive power is essential for a State goes without saying. The question is whether State sovereignty or supremacy is a supremacy of coercive power. The argument certainly does show that sovereignty cannot be defined as the *claim* to supreme authority, for different associations or communities may make conflicting claims to this effect, and the one that is sovereign is the one that can *substantiate* its claim. The question then becomes, what substantiates a claim to supreme authority? And the answer now suggested is, supremacy of coercive power.

3 OBJECTIONS TO THE POWER THEORY

I do not think it can be correct to say that State sovereignty consists in supremacy of coercive power, and that this and only this substantiates the State's claim to supreme authority. Supreme power is neither (1) a necessary nor (2) a sufficient condition for substantiating the claim. Let us look at each of these objections in turn.

(1) Supremacy of coercive power is not always *necessary* to substantiate a claim to supreme authority. This can best be seen in international relations. I grant that the State's claim to supreme authority within its own domain can usually be effective only if the State has at its command coercive power superior to that of any other association or group within its jurisdiction. There are occasional exceptions, but generally speaking the authority of the State and its laws will not last unless backed by superior power. This, however, was true also in the days before States were thought of as *sovereign* States. The idea of sovereignty has its point chiefly in regard to a State's relationship to authoritative bodies that are not located within its own domain, namely, other States and international authorities such as a universal Church or an international legal or political organization. It is therefore perfectly proper to point out that, in international relations, the concept of State sovereignty does not require a supremacy of coercive power. To say nothing for the moment of great and small powers, a few States, such as Liechtenstein and San Marino, have virtually no power at all, so far as international relations are concerned, yet they are sovereign States. No doubt they would not remain so if powerful neighbouring States chose to invade them and take over. Still, they do in fact exist as sovereign States with very little power by international reckoning.

Advocates of the power theory of sovereignty may say that these are not real or effective States; they are toy States, mere pretences that depend for their existence on the good pleasure of States proper, i.e. of powerful States. But consider where this line of argument would lead. The power theory is the view that sovereignty consists in supremacy of coercive power, that is to say, of power sufficient to allow a State to formulate and carry out its policies without having its freedom of action limited by any other body capable of exercising power. This will imply that only those States that are called Great Powers possess sovereignty.

I recall a discussion, at an international political science congress in 1961, between Professor Hans J. Morgenthau and Professor Raymond Aron. It was about the notion of a 'viable' State, not about sovereignty, but it can be applied to the power theory of sovereignty. Professor Morgenthau had written that Britain and France were no longer viable States, as they had been before the Second World War, because their freedom of action (e.g. in the Suez operation of 1956) was limited by the policies of the U.S.A. and the U.S.S.R. Professor Aron retorted that this implied that, of the 100 or more States in the present-day world, only two were 'viable' while the rest were 'non-viable'. Professor Morgenthau's thesis, he pointed out, was simply a novel, and misleading, way of saying (what everyone would accept) that there are now only two Great Powers and that Britain and France have ceased to be Great Powers. Nevertheless, Professor Aron added, Britain and France, and most of the others, manage to carry on as States and so are viable.

A holder of the power theory of sovereignty is obliged to say the same sort of thing as Professor Morgenthau said. Britain and France used to command enough power to give them freedom of action in carrying out their policies, but now their freedom of action is limited by the superior power of the U.S.A. and the Soviet Union; so that only Great Powers are really sovereign powers. The so-called sovereignty of other States is a pretence, depending on the good will of States that really have sovereign power.

Even a Great Power does not normally have complete freedom of action. Each of the two Great Powers in the present-day world has its freedom of action limited by the power of the other. That is what is meant by 'the balance of power'. The only kind of State that would have complete freedom of action would be one that controlled an empire over all those peoples with whom it had any effective contact, as Rome did in the first centuries of the Christian era. But the kind of limitation imposed by a balance of power is comparable to the territorial limitation on legal sovereignty. The legal authority of each State is confined to its own territory and is balanced by the equal authority of other States in their territories. Supremacy of legal authority does not mean an authority that is superior to any other existing authority, but one that is not inferior or subordinate to any other. In the same way the freedom of action of a Great Power is limited to its own sphere of influence and is balanced by the equal freedom of other Great Powers in their spheres of influence. Supremacy of power will mean power that is not inferior to that exercised by another State. It will accordingly be confined to Great Powers.

Obviously Great Powers do have a key position in world politics, and if the power theory were simply telling us that the formal equality of the legal sovereignty of all States is unreal when it comes to determining political issues in international relations, we should all agree. But this is not to explain the meaning of the concept of State sovereignty, which is not restricted to Great Powers and is not intended to be so restricted by those who interpret it in terms of coercive power.

(2) I turn now to the second leg of my criticism of the power theory. Supremacy of coercive power is not *sufficient* to substantiate a claim to supreme authority. This too can be illustrated from international relations, if we think of the circumstances in which a State will be given or refused recognition by other States. The exercise of effective control over a territory is a necessary but not a sufficient condition. The point of the criticism can be seen more clearly, however, if we look this time at the internal situation of a State.

Thomas Hobbes[1] in the seventeenth century employed an argument to the effect that power alone is not sufficient to substantiate political authority, or, as he put it, to constitute 'dominion'. Hobbes is often supposed to have held a power theory of sovereignty, but it seems to me that the main point of his theory is that both power and the acknowledgement of authority are

---

[1] See especially *Leviathan*, chaps. 20, 31.

necessary. Hobbes does take the view that the dominion of God is constituted by power alone; or at least he does so in some of his remarks about God. He says that the power of God is irresistible, and that this in itself both explains and justifies God's dominion over the whole world of nature, including mankind. But in the relations between man and man, no one person and no body of persons is in the position of God, namely of being able to exercise irresistible power everywhere all the time; and this fact is what makes the possession of power insufficient for political dominion.

Not that Hobbes is blind to the importance of power in politics. In one of his books[1] he compares the exercise of political authority to playing a trump at cards, and adds, 'save that, in matter of government, when nothing else is turned up, clubs are trumps'. (He probably thought of this trenchant epigram in recollecting a story about his father, who was a parson but not a shining example of the cloth. Cards were more to his taste than books. After sitting up late one Saturday night playing cards, he fell asleep during the church service next morning and apparently dreamt of card-playing, for he suddenly called out loudly, 'Clubs are trumps'.) Notice that Hobbes's own use of the phrase is that clubs are trumps in politics 'when nothing else is turned up'. If nobody has a regular trump card, a regular claim to political authority, such as popular consent or hereditary succession, then, but only then, power fills the vacuum.

Although Hobbes is fully apprised of the importance of power, he thinks it is essential to distinguish between power and dominion. He says that a captive or a slave is in his master's power, but is not thereby a *subject*, as is a citizen or a servant. A subject is one who acknowledges that his master has the right, not just the power, to issue orders, and that he himself is obliged, not just compelled, to obey. A captive or a slave obeys because he must, but if he is not chained and if he has the chance to escape when his master's back is turned, there is no reason why he should not take it. A servant, unlike a slave, works under a contract of service and is thereby obliged to do his master's will even

[1] *Dialogue between a Philosopher and a Student of the Common Laws of England.*

when he is not being watched; and according to Hobbes, a citizen differs from a captive in the same way. Of course men may become subjects of a new sovereign as the result of conquest, and Hobbes went so far as to say that if the people of a country are conquered in war and submit to the superior power of the conqueror, they become subjects, i.e. they are obliged to obey their new ruler, only because they can be presumed to have tacitly promised obedience and to be morally obliged through that promise. They have made the presumptive promise through fear of being killed, so that the promise has been extorted by force. But without the promise, Hobbes held, there would be no obligation and no dominion.

This looks like a distinction without a difference. Hobbes says that the subjects must be supposed to be obliged by a promise, made through fear of the conqueror's power, and that without the promise they would not be subjects. But is there any real difference between a captive who obeys from fear of his master's power, and a subject who is *said* to have given a tacit promise from fear of the conqueror's power? The distinction seems to be one of words only, as in John Harington's epigram:

> Treason doth never prosper: what's the reason?
> For if it prosper, none dare call it treason.

In fact, however, there is more to Hobbes's distinction than that. It would be a distinction without a difference only if the ruler could exercise his power all the time over everyone, that is, if he had the sort of universal, irresistible power that Hobbes has described God as having. Consider what coercive power usually means in a political context. It is not actual physical forcing, as when a stronger man presses a weaker man's finger on the trigger of a gun, thereby causing a third person to be shot. Some use of this kind of enforcement is made by officers of the State, as when a man who resists the police is dragged off to the police station, and as when convicted criminals are forcibly confined in one place by prison walls and bars. But more frequently the exercise of coercive power in a political context is inducing a man to obey your will from fear of the consequences if he does not.

Most men who are arrested 'come quietly', because they know that the police can frogmarch them if they do not. Now a ruler (or a body of rulers) who possesses coercive power, i.e. who has the means to make people obey him from fear of unpleasant consequences if they do not, cannot be applying that power to all of them all the time. He cannot have armed soldiers or burly policemen standing guard over all his subjects continually in order to compel them to obey his commands. We all know that in a crime thriller the villain is knocked out as soon as his eye or his gun wavers. If a ruler were to rely on coercive power alone, he would need to have a gun pointed vigilantly all the time at each of his subjects. As in a closed prison, there would need to be a permanent deterrent to escape or revolt. Even in a prison, unless the cells were never unlocked, the governor could not exercise power over the prisoners if he did not have the willing obedience of the warders. Even if a tyrant could have armed soldiers standing guard over every citizen, the obedience of the soldiers themselves could not be an enforced obedience. As David Hume[1] said, he must lead the soldiers, at least, by their 'opinion'; and as Plato[2] said long before, a band of robbers can be successful in terrorizing the populace only if there is an unforced loyalty among themselves. But in any event, a State, even a totalitarian State, cannot be run like a prison in most respects. To some extent at any rate, there must be a willing, or at least an uncompelled, obedience, which means an acknowledgement of authority. The laws of the State do indeed have the threat of force behind them; but if it were necessary to use that force on every occasion when there was the possibility of disobedience to the law, the system would break down. In fact, *most* people conform to the law because they recognize its authority and accept that they ought to obey.

A claim to authority may be acknowledged for different reasons. *One* reason (and it often applies) is the effective exercise of power. This is the truth that lies behind the theory that power sub-

---

[1] 'Of the First Principles of Government' in *Essays, Moral, Political, and Literary*.
[2] *Republic*, I.

stantiates authority. If a ruler (or a group) seizes power, he (or they) may at first be called a usurper, and later be acknowledged as sovereign. Those who are in his power may say: 'We submit; we accept your jurisdiction because you have the power.' This is what Hobbes has in mind with his tacit promise at the establishment of dominion by conquest. His point can be seen clearly in the signing of an instrument of surrender by the representatives of a nation defeated in war. That document represents Hobbes's 'covenant'. The defeated nation is committed, by a sort of promise, to abiding by conditions laid down by the conqueror. The conditions are accepted under duress, but the instrument of surrender is nevertheless expected to remain binding after the conqueror has withdrawn his troops.

So there is something in the power theory. But the effective control of power is not the only reason for acknowledging a claim to authority. Authority may be acknowledged on other grounds, such as hereditary succession or general consent (this last without any thought, because it may not be true, that the consent of a majority means the support of their power if it comes to a fight). And although the control of coercive power will often cause people to acknowledge a claim to authority, it does not always do so. If the power is exercised in a thoroughly brutal and unjust way, many of the people within the country may refuse to acknowledge the claim to authority, preferring resistance to submission even though the chances of successful resistance are slight. Other States similarly will tend to refuse *de jure* recognition to the new régime even though they may allow that *de facto* it has effective control.

It remains true nevertheless that the kind of authority which the State exerts cannot be exercised without *some* use of coercive power and without the ever-present possibility of falling back on enforcement when need arises. If men could be trusted always to act on decisions reached as among the Quakers, by finding 'the sense of the meeting', the exercise of power would not be necessary. This is what is implied in Marxist theory when it is said that eventually the State will 'wither away', i.e. that when men reach the stage of always guiding their action by reference to the common good, they will agree of their own accord and will not need to be compelled. In a religious community, and often in a well-conducted family, authority, whether it be the authority of one person or that of majority opinion, can be acknowledged and followed without the backing of power to enforce it. But in the general affairs of society this is not so, and therefore the State needs to possess coercive power to back its authority.

The authority of the State is of course the authority of law, and the laws of the State, as I said in the preceding chapter, differ from the rules of other associations and communities both by depending on force and by having sovereign authority. Force or coercive power is essential for law as well as for other aspects of politics, but the sovereignty of the State is an attribute of the authority of State law, not an attribute of the force or power that the State must wield in order to make its system of law or its policies effective.

4   POWER AND AUTHORITY

It is important to be clear about the distinction between power and authority, since they are often confused, in language as well as in thought. We speak of a statute giving a Minister 'power' to do this or that, when we mean giving him authority. Similarly we speak of going beyond one's 'legal powers' or acting '*ultra vires*', where again the word 'authority' would express our meaning more clearly. The looseness of usage appears right at the beginning of the theoretical discussion of sovereignty, in the work of Jean Bodin[1] in the sixteenth century. Bodin writes: 'Sovereignty is the absolute and perpetual power (*puissance*) of a State, . . . that is to say, the supreme power to command. It is here necessary to formulate the definition of sovereignty, because there is no jurist or political philosopher who has defined it, although it is the principal feature and the one most necessary to be understood in the treatment of the State.' He goes on to speak further of '*puissance souveraine*' and '*puissance absolue*', and so

[1] *Les six livres de la République*, I. 8.

gives the impression that sovereignty is a matter of power in the ordinary sense of the word. Now anybody has the power or ability to issue a command, but not everyone is authorized or entitled to do so in particular circumstances, and not everyone is either able or entitled to have his commands carried out. Does Bodin mean by 'absolute power' the ability to issue effective commands, i.e. the ability to have one's commands carried out? This would be power, properly speaking. Or does he mean the entitlement or right to issue commands and to have them obeyed? This would be authority. A reading of the whole of his account of sovereignty makes it clear that he means the second, but his use of the expression 'absolute power' suggests the first.

The most general meaning of 'power' is simply ability. This may be seen from the French term *'pouvoir'* and the Latin *'potestas'*, both of which are derived from the verb 'to be able' (*pouvoir, posse*). It is because of this general meaning of 'power' that we can use the same word for the power of a dynamo, will power, or political power. Let us call this meaning of the word, sense (1). When we speak of power in a social context, however, we are usually thinking of a specific kind of ability, the ability to make other people do what one wants them to do. Let us call this, sense (2). Power in sense (2) may depend on different things. A man may be able to get others to do what he wants, because he has the gift of the gab, or because they trust him for his wisdom or his integrity, or because he holds a special office, or because he has the strength to make things unpleasant for them if they refuse. All four of these reasons have a place in the exercise of political power, but the last of the four is especially prominent in situations of conflict. This last is coercive power, using the threat of superior force to make others do what you want them to do when they are unwilling. Let us call this, sense (3). Because coercive power is so prominent in political conflict, the word 'power', which at first simply meant ability of any kind, comes to acquire associations with enforcement. One can see this in the two French words *'pouvoir'* and *'puissance'*. Both nouns come from the verb *'pouvoir'*, but they have rather different connotations. *'Pouvoir'*, like the English word

'power', can be used either without or with associations of enforcement, having senses (1) and (2), as well as sense (3); but
'puissance' has a more definite tendency to carry overtones of
might and the possibility of coercion. Similarly Latin has the
two nouns *'potestas'* and *'potentia'*, both derived from the verb
'posse', but *'potentia'* often, though not always, carries overtones
of might, like *'puissance'*. On the other hand, *'potestas'* is often
used to mean 'authority', just as 'power' is, when we speak of
giving someone legal 'powers'. The reason for this should be
apparent from what I have said of the different grounds on which
power in sense (2) can depend. One of those grounds is the fact
that the person with power holds a special office. This means
that he has authority in virtue of his office. If a man holds a
position of authority, and is able in virtue of that position to get
others to do what he tells them to do, his power in sense (2)
is the exercise of authority. That is why the word 'power' can
be used to mean authority.

To have authority to do something is to have the right to do it.
Here we must distinguish two senses of the noun 'right'. Sometimes when we say that a man has a right to do something, we
simply mean that he may or is permitted to do it, that his proposed action is not forbidden by any law or moral rule, or that
he has been expressly licensed under some law to do actions of
this kind. In this sense of the noun 'right', a right is a freedom, a
licensed or permitted facility. I call it a 'right of action'. But
secondly, we often speak of having a right when it is a right to
receive something, and then it is also called a right against
someone else, who has an obligation to provide that to which the
first man has a right. Thus if Jones has a right to the £5 that
Robinson owes him, it is a right to receive £5, it is a right against
Robinson, and it corresponds to Robinson's obligation to pay up.
In this sense of the noun 'right', a right is a claim to something
due. I call it a 'right of recipience'. The French language marks
the distinction by usually employing the expression *'droit de'*
for a right of action, and *'droit à'* for a right of recipience. Now a
right of recipience need not be a right to receive something
material. It may be a right to be left undisturbed, to freedom

from restraint on doing whatever one chooses to do. This is the right to liberty, the right to be left alone by other people. It needs to be distinguished from a right of action, a freedom or licence to act, though usually, when we have a right of action, a freedom to act, we also have a recipient right to freedom from interference by others in the doing of what we are legally or morally permitted to do. Another non-material thing to which one may have a right of recipience is obedience. One may have a right to have one's orders carried out. Since this is a right of recipience, it is a right against some other person or persons, and the obligation which corresponds to the right is the obligation to carry out the orders.

Authority to give orders is this kind of right of recipience. We do sometimes speak of being authorized (less often of having the authority) to do something when we mean simply having a right of action, but with the implication that we also have a recipient right to be left undisturbed. If I have a driving licence, I have a right, or have been authorized, been given formal permission, to drive a car. Here 'I have a right to' simply means 'I may'. But when a Minister of the Crown is authorized (or 'empowered') by a statute to make regulations, this not only allows him to do something but also imposes an obligation on citizens to conform to the regulations that he may make. Thus it gives him a right to receive obedience to his regulations and not just a right to issue them. The authority to issue commands is not simply a right or permission to do something, as is a licence (or being authorized) to drive a car; it is also a right against those to whom the commands are addressed that they should do what they are commanded to do. It is a right to receive obedience, and it corresponds to an obligation on the part of others to give obedience.

In both senses, 'a right' or 'being authorized' may be thought of as a facility and so a power. I have already explained that the power to make other people do what you require may depend on the fact that you hold a special office. In virtue of holding that office you have the authority to make certain requirements of other people, and they do what you require because they

acknowledge your authority. Your authority, and their acceptance of it, are what give you the power to make them do what
you require. We can therefore think of authority as being one
species of power in sense (2), a species which is co-ordinate with
power in sense (3). The possession of coercive force is one way
of getting people to do what you require, one specific form of
power in sense (2); the possession of authority, provided it is
acknowledged, is another. It is therefore not surprising that the
word 'power' should often be used to mean authority.

A right of action may be thought of as a power in sense (1).
It is a facility, and so a sort of ability, to do something. We
express a person's right or permission to do something by saying
that he *may* do it, and in colloquial speech 'may' is often replaced
by 'can'. In French, '*puis-je*' is the regular way of saying 'may
I'. In 'correct' English, however, a distinction is made between
'may' and 'can'. The child who asks if he can have some more
cake is sometimes told: 'You don't need to inquire whether you
can. What you mean is to ask whether you *may*.' There is point
in the linguistic distinction. One often has the ability to do
something (whether it be to eat cake or to borrow or steal someone else's possessions) when one does not have permission to do
it, and at times one has the permission without having the
ability (e.g. to ride a friend's bicycle). Nevertheless a facility or
permit may be thought of as a kind of ability because it signifies
the absence of a barrier that might otherwise prevent one from
doing an action and so make one unable to do it.

The barrier is, however, usually a metaphorical one. A notice
that says 'Unauthorized persons are not allowed to enter these
grounds' may be accompanied by the physical barriers of a high
gate and walls, but the legal barrier referred to in the notice
does not actually render me unable to enter, as the gate and walls
do (unless I am agile enough to climb them). The barrier that
the notice conveys is a legal fiction, and likewise to regard a
permit or licence as conveying an actual ability is a legal fiction.
Any rule that says one must or may not do this and that, may be
understood as setting up a fictitious or metaphorical barrier or
bond, 'obliging' or 'binding' those to whom it is addressed,

limiting their freedom of action and so making them 'unable' to act otherwise than prescribed. This applies to moral as well as to legal obligations. When Martin Luther said 'Here I stand; I cannot do otherwise', it was not literally true that he could not, but he regarded his moral commitment as a bond which left him unable to act differently. Similarly the absence of a restrictive rule, or the waiving of a rule by the grant of permission, may be understood as the fictitious or metaphorical lifting of a fictitious or metaphorical barrier that might otherwise limit freedom of action, and so as 'enabling' one to do what otherwise one would be 'unable' to do. Since legal rules are backed by coercive power, the notice which forbids me to enter private grounds carries with it the threat that if I do enter, I may later be subjected by imprisonment to a real barrier on freedom of movement; but at the moment, if the notice is not accompanied by the real barrier of gate and walls, I *can* enter the grounds if I am prepared to risk the consequences. The fact that I *may* not enter is the fiction that I cannot.

Legal, moral, and conventional rules (including the rules of language) all convey fictitious bonds and absences of bonds, 'obligations' and 'rights', 'necessities' and 'possibilities'. It is not literally true that one is 'obliged' or 'bound', i.e. necessitated, to follow a rule of law, morals, etiquette, logic, or grammar, as one is literally bound to one place by a rope, or as one is obliged or necessitated by a landslide to make a detour in order to reach one's destination. These fictions of human thought and language have their point precisely because human beings are not and cannot be strictly necessitated in the whole of their behaviour but have, over an area of thought and action, the ability to choose between alternatives. It is only when one *can* in fact do (or believe) either of alternative possibilities that it makes sense to put up or remove fictive barriers with the words 'ought' and 'may'.

The relationship between the concepts of power and authority that I have so far considered are illustrated in the ordinary use of language. A further source of possible confusion, however, has been introduced into theoretical discussion by the frequent references of sociologists to a classification made by Max Weber[1] of three types of authority, or dominion (*Herrschaft*), rational-legal, traditional, and 'charismatic'. Rational-legal authority is the explicit form of what I have been talking about, a right to give orders and to have them obeyed, in virtue of an office held within a system of deliberately framed rules setting out rights and duties. Traditional authority exists where a person such as a King or a tribal chief holds a superior position of command in accordance with long tradition, and is obeyed because everyone accepts the sanctity of the tradition. The idea of charismatic authority is an extension of the meaning of the Greek word '*charisma*' (the gift of divine grace) in the New Testament. As Weber uses the term, it means authority resting on the possession of exceptional personal qualities that cause a person to be accepted as a leader. They may be qualities of saintly virtue, giving their holder religious authority; or they may be qualities of outstanding heroism, intellect, or oratory, that bring a following of loyal devotion in war, politics, or other kinds of enterprise.

Some writers on social theory have supposed that the third of these is authority in a different sense from that of the first and second, that it is a power or ability to command obedience, while the other two types are examples of a right to command. I think this mistakes the kind of difference that exists between the three types. Weber is describing different sources of authority, not different senses or meanings of the word. In each of the three types the person exercising authority is thought to have the right to issue commands, edicts, or precepts, and the right to be obeyed, but the right arises from different grounds. With rational-legal authority, the right comes from a set of rules that explicitly define rights and duties. With traditional authority, it again comes from a set of rules, but this time the rules are 'crescive', not 'enacted'; that is to say, they have not been deliberately formulated as being desirable or necessary, but have grown up gradually over a period of time in which a customary practice, what is usually done, has hardened into a normative rule, what

---

[1] *The Theory of Social and Economic Organization*, trans. A. M. Henderson and Talcott Parsons (London, 1947), chap. 3.

ought to be done. With charismatic authority, the right comes from the idea either that the leader's special qualities make him *fitted* to lead, or that they are a sign that he has been *authorized* by a supernatural being who is already credited with the right to command and to depute this right to vice-gerents on earth. A person who is thought to possess this kind of authority has the power or ability to command obedience only because his followers think he has the right to it.

Whenever authority is effectively exercised, the person in authority possesses power in sense (2). He is able to make other people do as he requires. But his power is not identical with his authority, nor is it the consequence of his mere possession of authority. It is the consequence rather of the acknowledgement of his authority by those whom he commands. In the case of charismatic authority such acknowledgement is a necessary condition of the existence of authority, so that one who has charismatic authority does also have power. This is not necessarily true of rational-legal or of traditional authority. Sometimes a man is invested with the authority of an office in accordance with formal rules or with tradition, but for some reason (e.g. popular rebellion against a King or a Government) his authority is not acknowledged by the majority of those who are supposed to be subject to it. He then has authority without power; he has the right to issue commands and to have them obeyed, but he is not able to acquire obedience. Authority therefore can exist without power; it is ineffective but it answers to the concept of having a right.

Power can exist without authority. It may then be that species of power in sense (2) which is also power in sense (3), coercive power. One who exercises coercive power is able to make others do as he wills, not because they acknowledge a right, still less because he has a right, but because they fear the consequences of disobedience. They are obliged or 'forced' to obey, in the sense in which a driver is obliged by a landslide to make a detour. Strictly speaking, they are not necessitated. They still have the choice of refusing to obey and taking the consequences, just as the driver need not make the detour if he is prepared to give up his purpose of reaching his desired destination. But since the consequences of disobedience, or of not making the detour, are usually thought to be even more undesirable than the alternative course of action, the latter is often said to be 'inevitable' or 'forced' upon us. We choose to adopt it, though unwillingly, but because the alternative offered is so much more contrary to what we should willingly choose, we think of it as not being a genuine alternative at all and say that we are compelled or obliged. The robber who brandishes a gun and says 'Your money or your life', compels his victim to give up the money because the alternative is one that most people would not dream of accepting. Effectively the threatened man is left with no real choice. He obeys because he must.

Obedience from the acknowledgement of authority is also said to be due to obligation, but here the choice is less reluctant, may indeed (in the case of charismatic authority) be made with enthusiasm, and is a genuine choice. Where it is not so, as in conforming to an unpopular law, it will commonly be found that the acknowledged authority goes along with the threat of coercive power, so that the obligation to obey authority is accompanied by the obligation (in the sense of compulsion) to avoid unpleasant consequences. The word 'obligation' has, in part, the same meaning in both uses, a requirement or 'necessity' to choose obedience. Strictly it is not a necessity in either case, since there is a choice. But the obligation of compulsion is much more like a necessity because we can hardly regard the choice as a genuine one. Where the obligation is purely due to the acknowledgement of authority, there is an open choice, and the idea of necessity or of being 'bound', that is suggested by the word 'obligation', is fictitious or metaphorical. Apart from this difference, there is also a partial difference in the meaning of the word 'obligation'. When I am obliged to do something from fear of unpleasant consequences, I am simply obliged to act. But when I am obliged by the acknowledgement of authority, I am not only obliged to act but am under obligation *to someone*. My obligation to him corresponds to his right against me. The fictitious 'bond' not only limits my freedom of action but 'ties' me to another person, who has the fictitious 'power' of a recipient right or claim. When

I am compelled, the wielder of coercive power has a real power over me, but we do not say that I am under an obligation to him or that he has a right against me.

5 SOVEREIGN AUTHORITY

Although it makes sense to speak of authority without power, political authority which ceases to be effective tends to lapse after a time even as authority. Since the prime purpose of political authority is to maintain order and security in matters of potential conflict, there seems no point in ascribing a right to issue orders unless they have a fair chance of attaining their purpose. If a system of State law is to be valid law, it must in general be effective. I do not of course mean that a failure to apprehend and convict some law-breakers renders a law invalid, but that the system as a whole must be effective. And since one cannot expect unanimous acknowledgement of legal authority or universal obedience in consequence of such acknowledgement, the authority of the law has to be joined with coercive power.

Why does the authority of the State have to be supreme? Why do we need the concept of *sovereign* authority? The answer to this question that is given by Hobbes is that in the absence of a supreme authority there will be chaos. If two persons or bodies of persons, each claiming authority, disagree, there is no way to resolve the disagreement except by setting up a supreme authority to decide disputes. Hobbes assumes that people cannot settle disagreements by rational discussion and by mutual consideration for each other's point of view. As we have seen, this is not always true. It is not true of a Quakers' meeting, or of any association or community based on love, or friendship, or mutual respect. Nevertheless it is true of much that goes on in social life, and this is why a final arbiter of disputes is needed if they are not to be settled by fighting, i.e. by seeing who has the greater coercive power.

It is not always necessary, however, to appeal to State arbitration for the settlement of disagreements. Consider an industrial dispute about wages. Employers and employees may be able to reach agreement among themselves through discussion. If they cannot reach agreement, then they may either resort to the use of such coercive power as the law allows, a strike on the one hand and a threat of dismissal on the other, or they may choose the method of arbitration, agreeing to accept the decision of an Arbitration Tribunal as authoritative. It should also be noted that there are matters in which dispute may be allowed to continue, without harm and perhaps with benefit. These are matters in which the dispute is in belief, with no immediate effects on action, or at least with no practical effects that constitute *conflict* in action. It may even be argued, as by John Stuart Mill,[1] that continuing disagreement and dispute in matters of belief is healthy, since it is the only way of approximating to the truth.

The argument for sovereignty in fact points beyond the Nation-State. The reason for having a supreme authority is to settle disputes without the use of force. The region in which we chiefly need this to-day is in the settlement of international disputes, and so there is everything to be said for giving up State sovereignty on external affairs in favour of a form of international sovereignty if a suitable one can be devised and can receive the agreement of all States. Here we again come up against the question of authority and power. We have seen that although it is possible to have authority without power, yet in practice, for political affairs, authority usually needs to be backed by coercive power. Hence the great difficulty of setting up international institutions with authority overriding that of the State. States may agree to accept certain international conventions, but when it suits a particular State to flout a convention, what sanction is there to prevent the convention from being treated merely as a piece of paper? The international authority needs to have the threat of coercive power in order to protect the rule of international law. But States are much more reluctant to place coercive power in the hands of an international authority than they are to sign conventions.

At the same time, so far as international law is concerned, it is by no means certain that the chief desideratum is the power

[1] *On Liberty*, chap. 2.

of sanctions for enforcement. Domestic law does indeed depend on sanctions, but it depends more on the general acknowledgement of its authority for other reasons. Some international lawyers tell us that the general acceptance of conventions and of the jurisdiction of international courts is more important than the establishment of an adequate international force to give effect to judicial decisions. Building up political institutions without regard to the realities of power is a risky business, but the acknowledgement of the authority of law and its procedures for settling disputes can go some way towards making it effective, and is certainly conceptually distinct from effectiveness by the use of coercive power.

IV GROUNDS OF POLITICAL OBLIGATION

1 PRUDENTIAL AND MORAL OBLIGATION

The authority of the State implies that those who exercise it have the right (of action) to issue orders and the right (of recipience) to have those orders obeyed, and that, corresponding to the second right, the citizens have a duty or obligation to obey the orders. In this chapter I shall consider the question: *why* does the citizen have a duty to obey the laws of the State? This is the problem of the grounds of political obligation.

Of course, there is one answer to the question that is simple and obvious: the citizen is obliged to obey the laws of the State because the State has sovereign authority. It follows logically that if the State is authoritative, i.e. has the right to issue orders to its citizens and the right to receive obedience from them, the citizens are obliged to obey those orders. The recipient right of the State to be obeyed by the citizens, and the obligation of the citizens to obey, are simply two different ways of expressing one thing, the metaphorical tie or bond between the two parties. This answer is formally correct but tells us virtually nothing, as when Hamlet is asked by Polonius 'What do you read, my lord?' and replies 'Words'. The answer evades the point of the question. In the case of our question about political obligation the answer takes the question to mean, 'Why is the citizen legally obliged to obey the law?' This question would indeed have no point at all, and could only be answered by a statement of the formal implications of the terms 'law' and 'legal obligation'. The citizen is legally obliged to obey the law because the law just *is* that which imposes legal obligation. To what else could there be a *legal* obligation except the law? But the original question, 'Why does the citizen have a duty or obligation (or, why ought he) to obey the law or the State?' was not meant in that sense. It meant, 'What reasons can be given for accepting the legal jurisdiction of the State?'

In Chapter III, Section 3, I said that a claim to authority can be acknowledged for different reasons. One reason is fear of the coercive power exercised by the person or body claiming authority; but there are other reasons too, such as general consent, or a rule of hereditary succession, or the possession by the claimant of special personal qualities. We now need to make a distinction of kind between reasons for acknowledging a claim to authority. (1) To acknowledge the claim from fear or dislike of the consequences of not doing so, is to admit a *prudential* obligation. It is to say that I ought in my own interest to obey; I 'had better' do so, or else it will be the worse for me. (2) To acknowledge the claim from the thought that it is right to do so, is to admit a *moral* obligation. It is to say that I have a moral duty to obey. So the question, 'Why ought I to (or, why should I) obey the law?' may be asked from either of two standpoints, and consequently it may be understood, and answered, in either of two ways. It may be asking for either of two kinds of reason for action. (1) It may presuppose the question, 'Is it in my interest to obey the law?' and so be understood to ask how it is in my interest. (2) Or secondly, it may presuppose the question, 'Is it my moral duty to obey the law?' and so be understood to ask why it is a moral duty.

Writers on moral philosophy used often to say that the word 'ought' has different meanings or senses when expressing prudential and moral obligation respectively. Nowadays it is more common to hold that the word has the same meaning but depends on different sorts of reasons in the two kinds of situation. This particular dispute in moral philosophy does not affect the distinction that I have drawn. It does not matter whether we say that the question 'Why ought I to obey the law?' has different meanings or the same meaning when asked from the two stand-points. What does matter is that different sorts of reason can be given in answer to the question. It is, however, worth noting that while the question in its present and in some alternative forms ('Why should I. . .?' 'Why am I obliged to. . .?') can be asked from either standpoint, this is not true when the noun 'obli-gation' is used. The question 'Why have I an obligation. . . .?' or 'Why am I under an obligation. . .?' cannot, so it seems to me, refer to a prudential obligation but only to a moral or a legal obligation. I have used the noun in speaking of a 'prudential obligation' to describe the situation where we may say a man 'is obliged' in his own interest to do something. But as I said in Chapter III, Section 4, such an 'obligation' is not an obligation *to* someone else, as is a moral or legal obligation. Not all moral or legal duties are of this kind, obligations *to* specified persons. For our present purpose, however, it is important to notice that some are.

I also said in Chapter III, Section 4, that the terms 'obliged' and 'compelled' are often used of action performed under duress, because the choice offered cannot be regarded as a genuine or effective choice when one of the alternatives is too unpleasant to be seriously entertained. We must not suppose, however, that this is always true of prudential 'obligation', or that if it is true for most people in a particular situation it is true for all. We certainly have a choice whether to follow a doctor's advice on diet even though we believe his prediction of the consequences of neglect. Most people threatened by an armed robber will feel that they have no choice, but a few will think differently. The fact that we often use the words 'ought' and 'should' to express prudential obligation shows that we think there is a choice. There would be no point in employing these terms if we thought that one course of action was inevitable. The armed robber does not say 'You really ought to hand over the money' (though he may well say 'You had better . . .'), as the doctor says 'You really ought to keep off alcohol'.

The question 'Why ought I to obey the law?' may be asked from the standpoint of prudence, and in that event it will be sensible to answer 'Because you will run the risk of imprison-ment if you disobey' or 'Because the law is intended to protect your interests along with those of other people'. There is no difficulty in providing an answer to the question in terms of self-interest, and one does not need the reasoning of a philosopher to discover it. Nevertheless answers to the question in terms of self-interest have figured in philosophical discussion of the grounds of political obligation, and the reason for this is that the standpoint of prudence has been confused with the moral stand-point. Because the same form of words can express different types of question, an answer in terms of self-interest has often been given instead of, or alongside, an answer in terms of moral duty.

Some people may be inclined to deny that political obligation has anything to do with moral duty. Let me try to show, then, than an answer to our question in terms of interest will not deal with the problem that has arisen in consequence of the discussion of the preceding chapter. Our problem is to find reasons for acknowledging the *authority* of the State. Authority implies two things: (1) it implies an obligation to obey the commands issued by the person or body vested with authority; and (2) it implies that that person or body has a right to issue the commands and a right to be obeyed. Now if we approach the problem from the standpoint of self-interest and say that the citizen ought to obey the rulers because it will be the worse for him if he does not, then we do indeed show that the citizen is obliged; we give him a reason why he ought to, or why he should, obey. But we do not show that the rulers have a right to make their demands or a right to receive obedience. We have pointed out that they have might, that they have the power to make things nasty for the citizen if he does not do what they require. But might is not right. Power may be said to oblige but not to confer a right. Furthermore, if we recall a point made earlier, we can note that the 'obligation' imposed by coercive power is not an obligation *to* the rulers, corresponding to a right against the citizen to receive his obedience. We can say that the citizen 'is obliged' to obey, but we should not find it natural to say that he 'has an obligation' or 'is under an obligation', and it would be clearly inappropriate to say that he is under an obligation *to* the rulers or that they have a right against him. On the other hand, if we give the citizen moral instead of prudential reasons for obedience, these can take the form of showing that he is not only obliged but is under obligation to the State, which correspondingly has a right to his obedience. And since we are seeking reasons for acknowledging authority, we need an account in terms of moral obligation and not in terms of prudential.

We can now see more clearly the point of the statement made in Chapter III, Section 3, that power alone is not sufficient to constitute authority. Power may make people feel (prudentially) obliged to obey, but it does not confer a right to obedience and so does not confer authority. We can also now see more clearly the point of Hobbes's contention, at first sight a curious one, that a conqueror acquires dominion only if his vassals are understood to have tacitly promised obedience. Their fear of his power does not make them subjects, or give him authority, unless there is the intermediate link of moral obligation created by a promise.

2   MORAL GROUNDS FOR POLITICAL OBLIGATION

Granting that prudential reasons for obedience cannot constitute reasons for acknowledging authority, does it follow that only moral reasons will suffice? If recipient rights and corresponding obligations towards those who have the rights may be either legal or moral, cannot reasons for acknowledging authority be legal as well as moral? Legal reasons may be given for acknowledging the authority of a particular law or of a particular ruler or official, but not for acknowledging the authority of the State as such or, to put it in another way, of the system of law as a whole. We have already noted that it is a mere tautology to say that we are (legally) obliged to obey the law because the law is what imposes legal obligation. The reasons for accepting legal obligation at all must be drawn from outside the system of legal obligation. We can, however, give reasons from within the system to justify obedience to a particular holder of authority.

I said earlier that, apart from fear of coercive power, one might acknowledge a claim to authority because the claimant had popular support, or satisfied a rule of hereditary succession, or had some special personal qualities. Popular support and special personal qualities may give rise either to prudential or to moral reasons. One may regard popular support as potential coercive power which it would be imprudent to oppose, or one may think that the consent of the majority constitutes a moral reason for acceptance. Likewise the success which is likely to attend a leader with outstanding personal qualities of character or intelligence may give rise to prudential or moral reasons for accepting his leadership; I may consider that his success will ensure my safety and prosperity, or I may consider that his aims, say a maximum of prosperity and justice for the whole society, are moral ends and that his personal qualities afford the best chance of achieving them. The case is different, however, when we take as our reason for acknowledging authority some rule like that of hereditary succession. Needless to say, my list of possible reasons was not an exhaustive one, and hereditary succession is not the only example of a reason provided by a constitutional rule. Now if one ruler succeeds another as his heir, or as having been duly appointed under some other constitutional rule, he is entitled to be obeyed because there is a law, a constitutional rule, to that effect. This gives us a legal reason for acknowledging the authority of the new ruler. Similarly a particular law has authority because it has been passed in accordance with the constitutional rules for making individual laws. But we may also ask why we should accept the constitutional rules themselves, and then we are asking for reasons outside the system of law for accepting the authority of the system. And in answering this question we may want to fall back on one of the reasons mentioned earlier, such as the consent of the majority or the best means of securing moral ends.

I have mentioned this complication in order to say just a word about the theory of divine right. In former days, one theory of the ground of political obligation was the theory that the sovereign was given his authority by God. There is little point in discussing the divine right of Kings nowadays because nobody in a modern State (leaving out of account pre-communist Tibet and some tribal kingdoms) would want to claim it. I shall therefore omit it in surveying theories of the ground of political obligation. The one matter that is still worth noting is that the theory of divine right, like others, made the legal authority of the King dependent upon moral authority. If it is assumed, as it was by the proponents of that theory, that morality depends on the will of God, then to say that a King is divinely invested with authority is to imply that his authority is moral and not merely legal. The basic problem in considering grounds for political obligation is to find moral reasons for obedience. It is felt that unless moral reasons can be found, there is no justification for acknowledging the State's authority. And once it was no longer thought plausible to say that a sovereign was invested with authority by God, it became necessary to find or return to other ways of giving a moral justification for political authority. The notion of charismatic authority likewise was originally one of divine authorization. The exceptional personal qualities of a religious leader like Moses or Jesus of Nazareth were taken to be signs that he had been invested with authority by God, and it was assumed that the will of God was the source of morality. A secularized idea of charismatic authority attributes to the leader himself superior capacities of moral judgement and of success in attaining what are taken to be moral ends.

Why does this problem of finding moral grounds for acknowledging authority apply specially to *political* obligation? Philosophers have not debated similarly the reasons for obeying the rules of other associations. They have produced theories to justify obedience to the laws of the State, but not to justify obedience to the rules of a club, or a school, or a Trade Union. The reason why the problem arises for political obligation is because of the universality and compulsory character of the State's jurisdiction. We have seen that compulsory acceptance of rules can apply, to a degree and for some people, in certain other associations, but the universality of the State's jurisdiction makes its compulsory character more pervasive and more evident.

Membership of most associations is voluntary. I can decide for myself whether to join and to accept the rules. If I do not like the rules, I need not join. If I decide to join, I do so freely, and in joining I promise to abide by the rules. But in the case of the State I have had no choice. I am a member, or at least am subject to the rules, whether I like it or not. It is therefore natural to ask why I should obey these rules if I have not freely chosen to do so. We should also note that some theories try to answer the question by saying that, despite appearances to the contrary, the situation is no different from membership of a voluntary association. They have argued that the obligation to obey the rules of the State arises from a sort of promise such as one gives when joining a voluntary association. Some other theories, but now outmoded like the theory of divine right, have compared the authority of the State with that of the head of a family; for membership of a family, like membership of a State, is not something we choose but something that is thrust upon us.

We are now in a position to survey those theories of political obligation which still retain, in my opinion, philosophical interest. I shall deal with five answers to the question: what are the grounds of political obligation? They are:
(1)   The State rests on social contract.
(2)   The State rests on consent.
(3)   The State represents the general will.
(4)   The State secures justice.
(5)   The State pursues the general interest or common good.

3 THE THEORY OF SOCIAL CONTRACT

The theory of social contract tries to justify political obligation as being based on an implicit promise, like the obligation to obey the rules of a voluntary association. A theory of contract proper has been held in different forms. I shall discuss three kinds of contract theory, and shall then turn in the next section to the theory of consent, which depends on a similar idea but is perhaps not intended to imply a contract or promise.

(a) Contract of citizenship

Theories of social contract go back a long way in history. Two explicit versions of the idea are formulated by Plato, and no doubt hints of it can be found in earlier writings too. The first form of supposed contract that I want to consider may be called a contract of citizenship, a contract made by each individual citizen with the State or the law. An implicit contract of this kind is described as the ground of political obligation in Plato's dialogue, *Crito*. The argument is put forward that if a man remains in a particular political society and enjoys its privileges, he is bound for his part to accept the obligations too. Socrates draws a metaphorical picture of the laws of the State saying to him that a bargain has been struck between them; by living in Athens he has implicitly promised to obey the laws in return for the privileges of an Athenian citizen.

A literal version of this doctrine applies to a man who acquires citizenship by naturalization. He applies for membership of the State, just as one may apply for membership of a voluntary association. He has weighed up the privileges and the obligations, and is prepared to accept the second along with the first. In many countries he is in fact required to give an explicit promise to accept the obligations, in the form of an oath of loyalty. Now since his legal position, once he has become a citizen, is supposed to be exactly the same as that of a citizen by birth, it seems reasonable to think that the basis of obligation is similar for both; and since the basis of obligation for the naturalized citizen is manifestly a promise to accept the obligations in return for the privileges, it seems reasonable to say that for the natural-born citizen too, although he has not given any explicit promise, the basis of obligation must again be quasi-contractual, the obligations being a fair return for the privileges.

Actually, however, the analogy does not hold good. Although the naturalized citizen is told that he has the same privileges and obligations as the citizen by birth, his consequent position is not precisely the same. In Britain, and in many other countries, a certificate of naturalization may be revoked if the person holding it is convicted of a serious crime. This means that his acquisition of the privileges of citizenship is conditional on reasonably good behaviour, and that fits in with the idea of a contract or bargain. But a citizen by birth is not, in most civilized countries, liable to be deprived of citizenship as part of the penalty for serious crime. And this reflects the idea that one cannot rightfully withdraw what has not been granted. The citizen by birth has not been granted citizenship; he has acquired it automatically.

Even if the two classes of citizens did have precisely the same status in regard to privileges and obligations, it would not follow that the ground of obligation was the same for both. This may be illustrated by a similar duality, in Britain at least, in the special military obligations of volunteer and conscript members of the armed services. A volunteer takes an oath of allegiance; he has chosen to accept the obligations of a soldier (or sailor or airman), and in signing the military oath of allegiance he explicitly promises to obey his superior officers. A conscript does not take an oath of allegiance; he has not chosen to serve, and so cannot reasonably be expected to give a promise; his military obligations are imposed on him by statute and are founded on his general obligation to conform to the laws. Yet once they are in the army, the volunteer and the conscript have exactly the same obligations and rights, although the grounds of obligation are clearly different.

What would the theory of contract of citizenship say of a man who thought that he received no benefit from being a member of the State, that he wanted neither the privileges nor the obligations? As Plato states the theory, it would say that in that case the man should have gone off to live elsewhere. Socrates represents the laws as arguing that, by remaining in Athens, he has shown that he prefers Athens to other city-states and therefore that he wants its privileges. This line of argument could not be applied so easily to-day, when many people are not free, as Socrates was, to become a citizen of a different State.

There are therefore two objections to the theory of contract of citizenship. First, it does not apply to natural-born citizens as it does to naturalized citizens. Secondly, the theory presupposes freedom to accept or reject the contract, and this freedom does not exist for many people nowadays.

(b) Contract of community

A second form of contract theory is discussed by Plato in the *Republic* (Book II), but not as a view that he himself accepts. This theory depicts men as being by nature egoistic, everyone out for himself. Everyone is therefore liable to suffer harm as well as to cause it, and so men make a compact or agreement with each other to set up laws for the regulation of their conduct. This, it is claimed, is the origin of society and of justice. The laws restrain our liberty to do as we like, but give us protection from injury by others. It is therefore in our interest to join in the compact. Having done so, we are obliged to obey the law because we have promised this in the agreement.

A similar version of the social contract theory is developed in more detail by Hobbes.[1] He too sees the natural man as largely an egoist seeking his own advantage. In consequence, if there were no organized political society, men would be in a state of war, in which everyone would be in danger of losing his life. We may suppose that in order to obtain security, men have made a contract with each other to give up their natural right to do as they please, and have invested a sovereign person or body of persons with authority to make laws regulating their action. The citizens are obliged to obey the law, both because they have promised to do so, and because the alternative to a politically organized society is the 'state of nature' in which every man goes in fear of losing his life. As held by Hobbes, the theory combines moral with prudential obligation. There is a moral obligation to obey the law because we have implicitly promised to do so. There is also a prudential obligation because the alternative is chaos; however restrictive the laws of the State may be, says Hobbes, any form of order is preferable to the chaos that results from the breakdown of the State. As in Plato's version of the theory, Hobbes represents the contract as having been made for prudential reasons, but he adds that our consequent obligation

[1] *Leviathan*, chaps. 13–18.

to obey the law rests both on the moral ground that we have promised and on a continuance of the prudential ground that led us to make the promise.

Several stock objections are made to this form of the social contract theory. One of them is more relevant to a contractual theory of ethics than of politics. If it is supposed, as the Platonic version of the theory in the mouth of Glaucon seems to suppose, that the idea of moral obligation itself depends on an agreement to observe moral rules, that in fact, as Glaucon says,[1] laws and agreements can come into existence only after a social contract has been made, then the theory is involved in a vicious circle. If agreements cannot be made in the 'natural' state of man before society has been organized by a social contract, it is impossible for a social contract to be made; if the idea of moral obligation depends on the conventions of law, men in the 'natural' state will have no conception of obliging themselves by a contract. There is, however, no need for a social contract theory to land itself in this difficulty if its aim is simply to explain political obligation. It can assume, as Hobbes does assume, that men in a state of nature are perfectly capable of making promises and contracts, and therefore of knowing what it is to put oneself under obligation; but because there is no security, without the organization of political society, that men will keep their promises when they can break them with impunity, it is desirable to set up a sovereign authority by means of the special device of social contract. For our present purpose, therefore, we can ignore the objection that a contractual theory of *moral* obligation is circular.

We can also ignore a second stock objection to the theory of social contract, namely that it is historically unsound because few States have in fact come into existence as the result of a social contract. Some of the philosophers who have held a social contract theory did think of it as an explanation of the way in which organized States first arose, but such an account, apart from being historically false, misconceives the purpose of a philosophical theory. An account of how things have come to be as they are, is a causal explanation of the type sought in scientific theory. A

[1] *Republic*, 359a.

philosophical theory attempts to supply justifying reasons for accepting a belief (in this instance, the belief that we ought to obey the law), not explanatory causes of the belief or its objects. As the proposed answer to a philosophical problem, the social contract theory should not be regarded as a theory of historical genesis. Hobbes at least is quite clear about this. He knows very well, and says so, that most States have come into existence as the result of conquest, not of social contract. But he adds, as we have seen in Chapter III, Section 3, that those who submit to a conqueror can become his subjects, i.e. can be under an obligation of obedience, only if they are assumed to have implicitly promised obedience so long as their lives are spared. Such subjects have placed themselves under a contract of citizenship (except that Hobbes regards it as a one-sided promise, which binds the subjects only and not the sovereign). Hobbes draws the admittedly mythical picture of a contract of community because this brings out more clearly the logical implications of sovereign authority and of the obligations of subjects. The purpose of the social contract theory in Hobbes is to illustrate what sovereign authority and political obligation mean, not to explain how States in fact arise.

A third objection, however, is more to the point. The theory, as put forward by Glaucon in Plato's *Republic* and by Hobbes, assumes that all forms of society are artificial, deliberately set up, and that man is by nature a solitary individual who thinks only of his own interests. The objection is that this assumption is psychologically untrue. Man is by nature 'a social animal'. Men have natural dispositions to association with their fellows, and to affection for kindred and other close associates.

The objection is sound in so far as the theory purports to account for the bonds of all forms of society. That form which Tönnies calls community rests on 'natural will', on bonds of affection and concern that grow up naturally among people who are close to each other, as for example in family relationship. But the main point of the theory is to account for the bonds of deliberately organized society, and especially the bonds of legal obligation in the State. We may agree that community is natural, but it does not follow that the State is natural. The real defect of the theory as presented by Glaucon and Hobbes is that it does not distinguish between community and the deliberately organized association of the State. It assumes that the only alternative to an organized State is a collection of psychologically isolated individuals, each out for himself and liable to come into contact with others only by way of hostile social relations. This is why I have given the name 'contract of community' to this version of the theory. As such it must be rejected. It can, however, be modified so as to avoid the objection, and it then becomes a different form of the social contract theory.

(c) *Contract of government*

Some social contract theorists have in fact distinguished between community (or 'society') and the State, and have spoken of a double contract, which we may call contract of community and contract of government. According to this form of the theory, men first contract with each other to join together in community (or 'society'), and then make a second contract in which they agree to set up a State and promise to obey its laws. A double contract theory of this kind was held notably by Samuel Pufendorf, writing a little later than Hobbes. The distinction between the two kinds of social union was not Tönnies' distinction between community and association, in which the very description of community implies that it is natural, not artificial. Pufendorf's distinction is between 'society', in a loose sense of the term, and that specific form of association that we call the State. Since 'society' in this loose usage includes community, the objection to a contract of community applies equally to the first half of Pufendorf's double contract. But we can drop this half of the idea, and simply retain the contract of government, which no doubt is what Glaucon and Hobbes were really after. The object of our inquiry is to find reasons for the obligation to obey the State, and if we think that the idea of contract can give us the answer, the only contract that we need to posit is a contract of government. We may say that community is a natural form of union depending on the social tendencies and needs of men, but that the organization of the State is set up deliberately, and that the obligations of law depend on an implied contract.

When so modified, the social contract theory avoids the objection I have made to a contract of community, but runs into a different one. The idea of a contract of government does apply to some instances of political rule. The founding fathers of the original American colonies did subscribe to a sort of social contract, because they supposed, under the influence of the political philosophy of the time, that this was the rational method of setting up a new State. Again, if we think of Hobbes's second category, a covenant of obedience made towards a conqueror by all the members of the conquered society, this answers well enough to the signing of an instrument of surrender by the representatives of a nation defeated in war. But then we need to ask, how can the promise of one generation bind later generations? The founding fathers of a State have voluntarily agreed to set up a form of government and to abide by its rules; and the leaders of a country defeated in war have, by signing the instrument of surrender, given a promise on behalf of all the citizens that the conditions laid down by the conqueror will be obeyed. Their acceptance of obligation has been voluntary, and in the second instance we may suppose that the general body of citizens have already agreed to accept decisions made on their behalf by their leaders. But the descendants of the generation which has promised are supposed to be equally obliged although they have not given or agreed to any promise. They have not freely chosen to accept their obligation.

It does in a way seem proper to say that the descendants of a defeated nation are bound by the conditions of surrender which were accepted by the earlier generation. The difficulty is that their obligation is not like that of a normal promise, which must have been freely given by all persons who are said to be obliged by it. For that matter, the original generation which accepted the conditions of surrender is in much the same boat. Normally a promise extorted under duress is not held to be binding, but this one is. It seems necessary to conclude that the agreement is not really a promise, as normally understood, but an analogous device of human invention to produce a continuing obligation after the coercive means of inducing prudential obligation have been withdrawn. At any rate the analogy which the social contract theory is designed to draw, between political obligation and the obligations of membership of a voluntary association, has broken down. Hobbes does, however, have a sound point about the obligation to obey a conqueror; it cannot rest simply on fear of his coercive power, once the major part of his armed forces has been withdrawn; and just as promises and contracts are devices for the smooth running of society, so surrender is a similar, though not identical, device for future peaceful relations. This means that the *ultimate* reason for abiding by the conditions, as for having the two kinds of device in the first instance, is general utility. Still, it does seem to me that the *immediate* ground of obligation to abide by the conditions of an instrument of surrender is similar to that of the obligation of promises. Although the obligation is not undertaken with that full freedom which applies to the giving of a normal valid promise, the actual device, like that of promising, is specifically designed as a means whereby obligations are undertaken.

In the case of the American colonies, the device used was literally that of social contract. The obligation of the original members, therefore, arose from a promise proper, and we cannot say that the obligation of their descendants is one of promise-keeping, since the descendants were not parties to the original contract. The obligation of an American citizen to-day to obey the laws of his State is no different from the corresponding obligation of a British subject. The theory of contract of government faces the same sort of difficulty as the theory of contract of citizenship; it can cover only a minority of relevant instances. The theory of contract of citizenship accounts for the political obligation of naturalized citizens, who accept it voluntarily by means of a promise, but not for the obligation of natural-born citizens, who have not accepted it voluntarily. Similarly the theory of contract of government accounts for the obligation of the founder generation of a particular State which happens to have been set up by this device, but not for the obligation of their descendants or of any citizens in States that were not founded in this way.

4 THE THEORY OF CONSENT

The doctrine of consent is a watered-down version of the social contract theory and is designed in part to avoid the difficulties facing the latter. It is simply that the authority of the State rests on the consent of the subjects. The idea of popular consent has played an important part in the development of parliamentary institutions in England. The process originated in the Middle Ages with the notion that property owners could not be taxed by the King without their agreement or consent. This led in the course of time to the appointment of representatives, who consented on behalf of the property owners to the raising of taxes and who took the opportunity, when they met for this purpose, to make grievances known to the King. Elements of this procedure are still retained in the usages of Parliament to-day. All Acts of Parliament state that the Queen legislates 'by and with the advice and consent' of Parliament. The idea is that the requirements of a statute are valid only if the representatives of the people have agreed to them.

This means that popular consent is essential for the authority of a *particular* law. The notion that consent supplies the ground of political obligation *in general*, is commonly associated with the political philosophy of John Locke,[1] though in fact Locke's theory includes also a kind of double contract (strictly, a contract and a trust) together with the idea, to be discussed in Section 6, that the State's purpose is to secure natural rights. However, he does talk as if the real point of the social contract lay in consent when he says that men remain in a state of nature, i.e. outside the bonds of political society, 'till by their own consents they make themselves members of some politic society',[2] and again when he says that 'no one can be . . . subjected to the political power of another, without his own consent'.[3]

Locke in fact thinks of this act of consent as an act of promising, so that his theory is still one of contract. The difficulty with the contract theory, as we have seen, is that most members of a

---

[1] *Second Treatise of Government*, especially chap. 8.
[2] Chap. 2, § 15. [3] Chap. 8, § 95.

State cannot be said literally to have given any promise. A watered-down theory of consent can try to meet this difficulty with the view that if a citizen *acquiesces* in the laws imposed on him, he may be taken to have consented; if a man, being born within a certain State, does not choose to leave, he may be taken to have consented to abide by its laws. This of course is the point that Socrates makes in Plato's *Crito* when he puts forward what I have called the theory of contract of citizenship. As stated in the theory of bare consent, however, the citizen is not regarded as having made a contract or given a promise.

The question that I now want to raise is this: if consent does not imply a promise, can it impose an obligation? It seems to me that the answer to this question is 'No'. Promising is a device for putting oneself under obligation by the use of a particular form of words.[1] To make a promise is to 'bind' oneself figuratively to the performance of an action or series of actions; it is to undertake an obligation. But mere failure to protest or resist surely does not create an obligation. It may perhaps be taken as an indication or sign *that* one has accepted authority but it does not afford a reason *why* one has done so. The idea of a contract does afford such a reason, since it is implicit in the notion of a contract that one promises to do something in return for an anticipated benefit. I am not saying that the benefit received or anticipated constitutes the reason why one is obliged to fulfil the promise; it is the reason why one has made the promise. The reason why one is obliged to fulfil the promise is simply the fact that the promise has been made. Nor do I imply that all promises are made for reasons of self-interest. A one-sided promise to benefit either the person to whom the promise is made or a third party, may be given for altruistic reasons; and for that matter, the benefit anticipated in return when one joins in the mutual promises of a contract, may be a benefit for a third party. The point is that the obligations incurred in making a contract are intelligible by reason of the benefits expected to accrue. But if we say that mere acquiescence imposes an obligation, so that bare

[1] This was first made clear by Hume, *Treatise of Human Nature*, III. ii. 5.

consent of this kind is undertaking an obligation, as is the giving of a promise, it is not intelligible why the person who acquiesces should be supposed to have undertaken an obligation. Of course, if he acquiesces because he fears the unpleasant consequences of resistance or protest, it might be said, as by Hobbes, that his acquiescence can be interpreted as a tacit promise, made for reasons of self-interest. But his acquiescence may be due to apathy or sheer failure to consider whether there is any alternative, and we cannot then say that he has a reason and that his acquiescence consequently may be interpreted as a promise. The device of promising has a purpose, and while it does sometimes make sense to speak of a tacit promise even though the device normally operates by the actual use of words expressing a promise, it surely does not make sense to speak of a tacit promise, or of undertaking an obligation without overt signs, if no reason can be assigned. A man might make an explicit promise without thinking of what he was doing and without having reasons for making it, and he might then be nonetheless obliged because of the conventions associated with this use of words. If, however, he has not actually made use of any form of words that would conventionally be called promising, we cannot attribute to him the undertaking of an obligation unless we know of good reasons why he may be supposed to have undertaken one.

In short, to say that no man can be subjected to political power without his own consent is a way of drawing the distinction between being compelled by coercive power and accepting authority. It is a way of saying that acceptance of authority is voluntary, while being coerced is not. As such, it has its point. But it does not give us reasons *why* we should accept the authority of the State, which is what we are looking for in seeking the grounds of political obligation. The theory of consent does not supply a ground of obligation unless consent is understood, as it is by Locke, to mean the making of a promise. If I am right, the doctrine of consent does not avoid the difficulties of the social contract theory. Either it is simply a form of social contract, or it cannot afford a ground of obligation at all.

5 THE THEORY OF THE GENERAL WILL

I take next the theory of the general will because this, like the theories of contract and consent, tries to make out that our obligation to obey the law is voluntarily assumed. It must not be supposed that this theory is either historically prior to, or logically simpler than, the theory of natural rights or justice, which follows in my order of treatment. The idea of the general will first appears in the work of Jean-Jacques Rousseau in the eighteenth century, while the theory of natural rights came into prominence in the seventeenth century. Furthermore, an important feature of the theory of the general or 'real' will is the view that morality, including rights, depends on the existence of organized society; in the hands of some of its advocates, such as T. H. Green, the theory begins as a criticism of the idea of natural rights.

Practically all versions of the general or 'real' will theory, whether in Rousseau or Hegel or the English Hegelians, Green and Bosanquet, are highly complex and rather obscure. The sketch of the theory that I shall give here may well be accused of being an over-simplified and even distorted parody, if taken to represent the view of any important philosopher. This book is not a history of political philosophy but a simplified indication of problems and attempted solutions. It should not be thought that what I say in this section is an accurate interpretation of the view of any one political philosopher, or that the important insights of Rousseau or Hegel are disposed of by my criticism. In the case of Rousseau, indeed, it may be held that his theory is not intended to give the grounds of political obligation in actual States, since his purpose is the different one of working out a hypothetical or ideal state of affairs which would, if it were practicable, reconcile freedom with authority.[1] As against that interpretation, however, there are features of Rousseau's main work on political philosophy, *Du Contrat social*, which suggest that he is dealing with the actual as well as the ideal. The fact

[1] See, for example, the admirable discussion by Professor John Plamenatz in *Man and Society* (London, 1963), Vol. I, pp. 391ff.

is that he is not a consistent writer. However, I am not claiming to give an accurate interpretation of Rousseau or of the other philosophers I have mentioned, but only an outline of an interesting type of answer to the question of why we are obliged to obey the law.

The view is that we ought to obey the laws of the State because they represent the general will. What is meant by the general will? One might suppose that it means either the will of all the citizens or the will of the majority, but obviously the first of these will not do. If the general will meant the will of all, the theory would not have given us an answer to our question. For if everyone wanted the same thing to be done, there would be no problem. 'Everyone' includes me, and if the State is doing what I want to be done, I shall not ask why I should join in. The question is raised only because the demands of the State often go against the wishes of an individual, who in consequence is disposed to ask: 'Why should I do what the State requires, when I do not want to?' In any event, if the State is to act only when there is unanimity among all the citizens, it will have to wait until the millenium before it does anything at all.

Let us turn to the more promising alternative suggestion that the general will means the will of the majority. Why does majority opinion lay an obligation upon the dissident minority? Suppose that most people want the State to do something or other, e.g. to build earthworks so as to prevent flooding, but I do not, because I live on the top of a hill and do not want to pay taxes for earthworks that will be of no benefit to me personally. Why should I fall in with the majority? What is the justification for accepting a majority view? One reason that might be suggested is that a majority is more likely to be right than a minority. If two heads are usually better than one, then thirty million heads are probably better than twenty million. Probably, but not certainly. Two heads are not always better than one. Some heads have better brains in them than others. If fifty sheep take it into their heads to go one way when their shepherd thinks they should go the other way, the shepherd is not likely to be impressed by the argument that fifty heads are better than one. Still, when all the heads belong to human beings, it is not easy to say who are the sheep. There is often no means of knowing, especially in political affairs, who is likely to be right. We also need to ask, right about what? In my example of building earthworks to prevent flooding, the difference of opinion arose from what people wanted. If politics is to be concerned with what people want, then, brains or no brains, a man can usually be expected to know what he himself wants; so that if the ideal, but unattainable, aim is to satisfy the wishes of all, we shall come nearer to it by satisfying the wishes of a majority than by satisfying the wishes of a minority.

In fact, however, the theory of the general will is not referring to the wishes of the majority. Rousseau, for example, says that the general will is always right.[1] This sounds as if he accepted the view that 'fifty million Frenchmen can't be wrong'. But he does not mean that the majority are always right. He knows they are not, and he wants his general will to be something superior to the fallible opinion of the majority. If we ask 'right about what?' the answer that we receive is 'right about the common good (or common interest)'. The object of the general will is the common good, not what any particular people happen to want for themselves. The common good is taken to be the aim of moral volition, and the general will is the will that each man has as a citizen or moral agent, not the sum of particular wants that each has as a non-moral individual thinking of his own interests in isolation from the interests of others.

Now if the theory of the general will were simply saying that we ought to obey the laws of the State because they seek to promote the common good and that this is the proper aim, or one of the proper aims, of each of us as a moral agent, it would be nothing more than a version of the common good theory, which I have placed last on my list, and which is a straightfoward utilitarian theory of political obligation. But in talking of a general or real *will*, the theory goes farther than that. It holds,

[1] *Contrat social*, II. 6. He qualifies this statement (in the second, revised version of the book) by adding 'but the judgement which guides it is not always enlightened'.

not simply that the common good is what we morally ought to aim at, but that this is what we 'really' *want*, and that therefore the State, in pursuing a moral aim and in requiring, sometimes forcing, us to give effect to that aim, is getting us to do what we want, despite appearances to the contrary. How does the theory reach this paradoxical conclusion?

I said earlier that we might justify the following of majority preference if we thought that political decision should approach as near as possible to an ideal aim of giving everybody what he wanted. Now a person may want something which is not good for him; and it might be argued that what is good for someone is what he *would* want if he had complete wisdom about the consequences of satisfying alternative possible wishes. He thinks that what he now wants will satisfy him, but this is because he is ignorant of some consequences. In fact it will not give him lasting satisfaction. It is only an apparent good. His real good, what would give him real or lasting satisfaction, is what he would want if he had more wisdom. Holders of the general or real will theory then take the step of saying that his real good is what he 'really' wants though he does not know it. They also argue that a man's real good or interest must be in harmony with that of other men, since a conflict of interests is harmful to all concerned. Such a harmony could be secured if the interests of all were the aim of each. This common good, or general interest, is what we ought to pursue; it is the object of a rational, real, or general will, and so is the real good of each individual. Since the State aims at securing the common good, the State or the law is the concrete expression of the general will. We ought therefore to obey the State, and if we do so we are following our real will, a will that is general or common to all the members of the State. If a particular individual does not understand what he 'really' wants and is unwilling to fall into line, the State is justified in forcing him to conform.

There is more than one unwarranted jump in this train of argument, but I shall confine myself to three objections. First, the theory assumes that the Government knows better than the individual what he really wants. 'The man in Whitehall knows best.' Now the man in Whitehall may know more than I about the causal effects of different policies. His knowledge of economics, for instance, may enable him to say that if the rail services are electrified they will be twice as quick and will cost twice as much. I know little of economics and am prepared to defer to his superior knowledge in accepting his conclusion. It says nothing about my wants. But suppose the man in Whitehall then adds that a quick service is preferable to a cheap service, and that therefore the railways ought to be electrified. There is no reason for me to treat his opinion on this issue as being knowledge of what I really want. If I do want a quick service rather than a cheap service, it will be rational for me to agree that the railways ought to be electrified and that I ought to pay more taxes or higher fares. But if I decide that I want a cheap service rather than a quick one, it is no use saying that I 'really' want a quick one because the man in Whitehall thinks it will be best for me. Perhaps it will, or perhaps most people want it, and either of those circumstances may be a good reason for going ahead with the policy and requiring me to join in the cost. The fact remains that I do not want it.

Secondly, the theory holds that everyone really wants the same things; it makes no allowance for differences of taste. It assumes that fundamentally human nature is always the same. But if, as is presupposed by the theory itself, people differ in their knowledge, why should they be supposed not to differ in their wishes? Indeed the mere fact that they differ in their intellectual capacities makes it likely that they will have different tastes in consequence of their different capacities, and this of course is what we find.

Thirdly, the theory identifies moral obligation with interest. It says that what I ought to do is what I really want to do. It assumes that there can be no obligation other than prudential obligation, and this is why it has to make the absurd assumption that everyone wants the same things. Now there is nothing absurd in saying that everyone shares a common set of moral obligations. It is perfectly sensible to say that everyone has a moral obligation to promote the common good, i.e. to serve other people's interests as well as his own, so far as he can. We can make this moral obligation the ground of political obligation, as is done by the utilitarian theory. In a way, the general will theory is doing the same thing, as I said earlier, but this simple, straightforward thesis is confused and distorted in the general will theory because it is supposed that one can be obliged to do something only if it is in one's own interest, a means to what one chiefly wants. The mistake is a common one, but in the case of the general will theory it is aided by the further supposition that a solution to the problem of political obligation must take the form of showing that somehow the State is a voluntary association.

6   THE THEORY OF JUSTICE

The three theories that I have so far considered all try to make out that political obligation is voluntarily undertaken and is grounded on this voluntary acceptance itself, independent of aims or consequences. The two theories that remain take a different line. They concentrate simply on the purposes of the State and hold that we are morally obliged, generally speaking, to obey the State because the State is a means to the fulfilment of moral ends which are themselves the objects of moral obligation for everyone. In principle, therefore, the theory of justice and the theory of general interest or utility take the same sort of form, and my own opinion is that they need to be combined. They have, however, been held separately, partly because earlier ideas of the purposes of the State were confined to the negative function as I explained in Chapter II, Section 5(c), and partly because the utilitarian theory takes the concept of justice to be comprehended in that of utility. It will therefore be convenient to consider them separately in the first instance.

According to the theory of justice, our obligation to obey the laws of the State depends on the fact that these laws are intended to secure justice or moral rights. One version of the theory speaks of 'natural rights', a conception that plays an important part in the political philosophy of Locke, who also, as we have seen, held a doctrine of social contract or consent. It is of course possible to think that there is more than one ground of political obligation, and thus to combine two or more theories.

The theory of natural rights maintains that men have certain absolute moral rights, such as the right to life, to liberty, and to the opportunity to pursue happiness. (Locke in fact made life, liberty, and property his three cardinal rights; but he was clearly uneasy about joining a natural right to property with the other two, for whereas it seemed to him self-evident that all men have a natural right to life and liberty, he thought it necessary to produce an elaborate argument for the view that there is also a natural right to property. The American Declaration of Independence, which was much influenced by Locke's idea that the purpose of political society is to protect natural rights, substituted 'the pursuit of happiness' for 'property' in its list of three cardinal rights.) These rights were called 'natural' because they were thought to be derived from 'natural law' or the law of God, but there is no need to include metaphysical or theological preconceptions in the idea of such rights. 'Natural law' was simply a way of describing principles of morality. They involve duties and rights, as does positive law, and the adjective 'natural' was used in order to contrast moral principles and rights with artificial or man-made laws and rights. Some rights are plainly man-made, such as the right of certain persons in Britain to an old-age pension of a fixed amount of money per week. This right would not exist if the State did not grant it. When it is said that the right to life, or the right to liberty, is a natural right, this means that it does not depend on man-made laws but is a right irrespective of whether the State or any other organization guarantees it.

Locke's view was that the State is designed to guarantee and protect natural rights. If we think that the notion of justice includes more than what Locke had in mind as natural rights, we may expand his doctrine and say that the State is designed to guarantee justice, i.e. established rights plus fairness. We may then say that if the State effectively carries out this function, we are thereby under an obligation to support it and obey its rules. On this view, political obligation depends on our moral obligation to respect rights and pursue justice.

So-called 'natural' rights are a species of moral rights of recipience, which go along with 'natural', i.e. moral, obligations. To say that a man has a moral right to life and liberty is simply an alternative way of saying that other people have a stringent moral obligation not to take his life or interfere with his liberty. 'Natural rights' or 'rights of man' or 'human rights' are moral rights attributed to every human being and corresponding to 'natural' or moral obligations which everyone has. But since some people do not in fact respect the rights of others, it is expedient to have an agency, the State, which will protect rights, if need be by force. The theory takes for granted that everyone has a moral obligation to respect rights and promote justice. In consequence it is morally obligatory to take the necessary means to that end. If the State serves as such a means, it is morally obligatory to give the State our support. Political obligation is treated as a form of moral obligation, the State being regarded as a necessary means to a moral end, the securing of justice.

It should be noted that this theory of the ground of political obligation implies that our obligation holds good only if the State does secure justice. If the State acts unjustly, it is not a means to a moral end and it forfeits its right to be obeyed. Locke deliberately intended this consequence. He wanted to show that it was justifiable to rebel against the existing rulers if they were pursuing unjust policies. Locke would also say, however, that, human nature being what it is, there is little chance of securing justice to any appreciable degree unless we have a State to enforce it. So that, if we live under an unjust government, his view would be that we are entitled, indeed obliged, to replace it by another government which will aim at securing justice. Mere rebellion by itself is not warranted, but only rebellion which aims, with reasonable hope of success, to replace an unjust by a just régime.

The theory of natural rights has been criticized on the ground that no rights are absolute and that natural rights are a myth. There is in fact no need for the theory to maintain that natural rights are absolute, i.e. that there are no circumstances in which a man loses them. Most of us would agree that a criminal forfeits his right to liberty for a time; and it may be argued that a murderer who deliberately and coolly takes the life of another thereby forfeits his own right to life, though this does not necessarily imply that the State or anyone else ought to execute him. Locke undoubtedly thought that natural rights are forfeited by one who breaches the natural rights of others. Some advocates of the doctrine of natural rights have called them 'inalienable' or 'imprescriptible', but what they have meant is that moral rights cannot be lost merely by legal enactment. A man may forfeit moral rights if he deliberately breaches the similar moral rights of others, and the law may give effect to this by listing crimes and imposing punishments. What it cannot (morally) do, according to the theory, is to deprive a man of his moral rights for non-moral reasons. All this is simply reiterating that moral rights and obligations do not depend on law and that legal obligations must depend on moral reasons if they are to be morally acceptable.

The second objection, that natural rights are a myth, may take either of two forms. (1) It may mean that the theological or metaphysical presuppositions of Locke and others are mythical. To this we may reply that, as I have said earlier, the natural rights theory can stand without such presuppositions; the word 'natural' here simply means non-artificial, and the rights concerned are moral as distinct from legal rights. (2) The objection may be understood, however, as a denial that there can be such things as moral rights distinct from legal ones. It may be said that 'rights' is a legal term and cannot properly be used to refer to anything other than legal rights. In reply to the objection in this form, we must allow that the term 'rights' is initially used in the context of law, but it has come to be used, by analogy, outside the field of law, and I do not see why the extended use should be called improper. We should all agree that there are moral as well as legal obligations. Legal obligations often correspond to legal rights, and therefore it is quite natural to think of certain stringent moral obligations as corresponding to moral rights. This is hardly more than saying that the obligations are stringent obligations and that they are obligations *to* other persons. To say that *A* has a moral right against *B* is just another way of saying that B has a stringent moral obligation to A. The meaning of the two statements is perhaps not quite the same, for often the point of saying that A has a moral 'right' is to express implicitly the view that it ought to be turned into a legal right, i.e. that the obligation of B towards A ought to be enforceable by law. Certainly one of the main points of issuing declarations of 'the rights of man' or 'human rights' is to urge that these moral rights be given legal protection and so be turned into legal rights. In that case, the objector may think, it would be less misleading to speak of interests that ought to become rights instead of calling them moral rights. But if he agrees that B does have a stringent moral obligation towards A, this is all that is required by the natural rights theory. As an account of the grounds of political obligation, the theory says that the State is a necessary means to the fulfilment of certain moral obligations that we all have, and therefore we are morally obliged to give it our support.

In any event, all these objections to the idea of natural rights disappear if we extend the natural rights theory, as I have done, into a theory of justice. Few philosophers will deny that justice is a moral as well as a legal notion. Utilitarians would object to the theory of natural rights and to the theory of justice alike, on the ground that these notions are both concealed forms of the idea of utility. The ultimate and comprehensive principle of morality, in their view, is the promotion of the general happiness; and justice is a means to that. My own opinion is that the idea of justice cannot *wholly* be subsumed under that of utility for the general happiness, but this is a question that I shall leave for discussion in Chapter VII, Sections 1 and 4. Meanwhile we can turn to the utilitarian theory of the ground of political obligation.

7   THE THEORY OF GENERAL INTEREST OR COMMON GOOD

This theory is held by Utilitarians, who take the view that all moral obligations depend on their utility for promoting the general happiness or interest. The State is a necessary means to securing a substantial part of this moral end, and therefore we are obliged to obey the law as an essential condition of fulfilling our general moral obligations. The State carries out its purpose by laying down laws, backed by force, requiring everyone to refrain from actions (crimes and torts) that harm the common good, and to contribute in taxes and other imposts to the upkeep of services (such as defence, public utility, and social services) that promote the common good. As with the theory of justice, it follows from the utilitarian theory that if a particular Government is harming instead of helping the promotion of the common good, it loses its right to obedience.

I imagine that everyone would accept the common good theory as providing *one* of the grounds of political obligation. Objection would be raised only to the thesis that it provides all the grounds needed. We have seen that the general will theory includes the idea of the common good as the object or aim of the State. Both the general will theory and the theories of contract and consent, however, would say that this is not sufficient because political obligation must have been voluntarily undertaken. It is not in fact true of most citizens that they have, in any straightforward sense, voluntarily undertaken their obligation to obey the State, but there is point in the contention that consent in some sense is a necessary addition both to the theory of common good and to the theory of justice. I shall consider this in the next section. Meanwhile we may turn to an objection to the common good theory that naturally suggests itself from our discussion of the theory of justice.

Both the theory of justice and the theory of the common good ground political obligation on the functions of the State in pursuing a moral end. When I dealt with the functions of the State in Chapter II, Section 5 (c), I said that its negative function was to preserve order and security, and that its positive function was to promote welfare and justice. Each of the two theories that we are now considering would claim to cover the negative function. The theory of justice would say that this function is the protection of established rights, one aspect of justice. The common good theory would say that the negative function is to prevent harm to the common good. What of the positive function? I do not think it can be said that the further *promotion* of welfare is an aspect of justice, so that if we accept the theory of justice as giving one ground of political obligation, we must add the theory of common good as specifying another similar ground. We should then have the composite theory that political obligation is grounded on the moral character of the functions of the State, these being both the securing of justice and the promotion of welfare. The common good theory, however, would say that it already provides for all functions, since the concept of justice is comprehended under utility. Just as the protection of established rights is a method of preventing social harm, so the redistribution of rights in terms of fairness is a form of promoting the general happiness. Take reward and punishment, for example. According to utilitarian theory, reward is appropriate only for such achievements as are useful to society, and it is appropriate because they are useful and because the encouragement of them by this incentive is useful; punishment is appropriate only for such actions as are harmful to society, and it is appropriate because they are harmful and because the discouragement of them by this sanction is useful. This view obviously has a certain plausibility. As I have already mentioned in the preceding section, I myself do not think that utility can account for all the ideas included in our concept of justice, and therefore I consider that both the theory of justice and the common good theory need to be combined in giving the grounds of political obligation. Those who think that justice is comprehended in utility can adopt the common good theory alone.

8   OBLIGATION AND AUTHORITY

Both theories, however, still have to meet the contention of the contract, consent, and general will theories that it is not enough to refer to the moral functions of the State. We have seen that it is a mistake to say, of most citizens, that they have, in any straightforward sense, voluntarily undertaken their obligations to the State. The State is not a voluntary association. Nevertheless the contention has point, which may be brought out in the following way. Authority, or a right to give orders, it may be said, must have been granted by people in a position to grant it. The fact that an agency pursues a moral end does not by itself oblige others to give it their support. Otherwise we should have to say that our general moral obligation to be charitable implies an obligation to support any and every charitable association, instead of leaving us free to fulfil our moral obligation in whatever way we choose.

The theories of justice and the common good can give a partial answer to this objection by reminding us that they treat the State as a *necessary* means to fulfilling some of our general moral obligations, and it is this necessity which directs our general obligation into the channel of political obligation. The State, with its system of enforceable law, is a necessary device for securing essential rights and interests, and this fact, together with our acknowledged moral obligation to promote justice and the common good, obliges us to give the State our support.

This is not, however, a complete answer to the objection since it does not meet the point about authority or a right to give orders. I said in Section 1 that the problem of the grounds of political obligation could not be solved in terms of prudential obligation because that would show only that we were obliged to act, not that the State had the right, implied by the idea of authority, to give orders. Now an account of political obligation in terms of the moral functions of the State does not indeed make political obligation prudential, but it does show only that we are obliged to act and not that the State has authority. The answer to the objection which I have put forward comes to saying that we have moral obligations to the members of our national community (as we have, though often in a different degree, to other persons also), that some of our moral obligations to other members of our national community can be fulfilled only through using a necessary device, and that therefore we are 'obliged' to use the device, just as a man is 'obliged' to make a detour if, owing to a landslide, that is the only way to reach his destination.

The 'obligation' to use the device of the State is not a prudential obligation, because the end which it serves is not self-interest but the common interest together with justice. Nevertheless its obligatory character is that of being obliged by the exigencies of a situation and not that of being under an obligation *to* some person or body that has a corresponding right. Of course we are under an obligation to the other members of our community, but when we are obliged to obey the State as a necessary device for fulfilling some of our presupposed obligations to others, this does not mean that the State has been given a right to issue orders and to have them obeyed.

We can see therefore that it was not superfluous for the theory of the general will to add something else to the idea of promoting the common good, or for the theories of social contract and consent to fix their attention upon the idea of authorization. An account of political obligation purely in terms of the moral functions of the State is not enough. What should be added? If we were to add the idea of a social contract, we could say that the contract is an agreement to use the device of the State for promoting moral ends; it would constitute a form of authorization that the State should act on our behalf. But the objections to the contract theory will hardly allow its reintroduction at this point, though I shall suggest in the next section that the idea of social contract does have some place in the institutions of a democratic society.

What of the weaker notion of consent in the sense of acquiescence? I think the addition of this suffices for giving the State a right to act as it does. I said in Section 4 that the theory of consent in the weaker form does not afford a ground of obligation, but in the composite theory that I am now building up, the *obligation* does not come from consent. The obligation comes from the presupposed moral obligation to promote the ends of justice and the common good together with the recognition that the State is a necessary means to those ends. All that consent is required to do is to allow the State to act as the agent of the citizen body. This need not involve an explicit contract. For most of us, the State is a *fait accompli*, already exercising its functions; but if we recognize the necessity of it for the securing of moral ends, and acquiesce in its continuing to exercise its functions, we thereby permit it to act as the agent or channel through which we are to fulfil part of our moral obligations. The consent adds to the State's power the authority or right to give orders, and since it is acting as an agent or channel for moral obligations, our obligations to fellow-citizens are channelled into an obligation to follow the arrangements made by the State.

9 THE EXTENT OF POLITICAL OBLIGATION

What follows in regard to the extent of political obligation? Obviously it does not follow that political obligation is absolute, i.e. that subjects are obliged to obey anything at all that the State may decree. On the contrary, since their political obligation depends on pursuing the ends of justice and the common good, they are not obliged unless the State's laws are effectively directed towards these ends.

But who is to judge whether the State's laws are effectively directed towards securing justice and the common good? The man in Whitehall, the majority, or each individual for himself? If any individual thinks that a particular law is unjust or harmful to the common weal, is he morally entitled to disobey it? If we answer that he is, the whole system will become unworkable. If the State must win the approval of *all* citizens for *every* law, no laws will be passed; and yet it will be plain to everyone that a number of rules of some sort need to be made and accepted, although there is not unanimity on the details. We are faced again with the problem of the general will. And here I think we may say that, in a democratic society, something like a social contract can properly be assumed. If the State's system of law *as a whole* is directed towards the approved ends of justice and the common good, there is a convention that whatever is decided in detail should be accepted as binding. This convention is acceptable only if those who take the decisions are authorized to do so by the general body of the citizens, and since unanimity is impossible even for that, majority opinion (either in the community as a whole, or, with large States, in constituent units) is taken to be the best approximation to the general will.

I am suggesting that something like a social contract does operate, in a democracy, for the acceptance of *particular* laws, provided that these can properly be said to represent the general will, as being authorized by the majority, with due regard to the differing views of the minority. The minority may be taken to have consented to accept decisions so reached, as representing the general will. My suggestion is that the *general* obligation to accept the authority of the State depends on the State's pursuit of the moral objectives of justice and the common good; and that the *particular* obligation to obey a specific law, with which one may disagree, can be regarded as contractual, depending on the convention of accepting majority decision.

Now I objected to the idea of social contract, when offered as the ground of political obligation in general, that one could not properly speak of a promise in the case of most citizens. Cannot the same objection be made again? Where is there a promise to abide by the decision of a majority of representatives, or of a Government? I think we can say that such a promise is implicit in the procedure of an election (or of a referendum). If one takes part in an election, or in a vote (whether it be a referendum of the whole populace or a vote in a legislative assembly), one can be assumed to have agreed to the presuppositions of voting procedure, namely that the majority opinion will be treated as decisive. To take part in an election is implicitly to promise to accept the majority verdict. If this is correct, it will follow that a compulsory requirement to vote in elections is contrary to the necessary condition of a promise that it be given voluntarily. Compulsory voting has occasionally been adopted in some States, and someone may say that this fact is an argument against the hypothesis that taking part in an election presupposes a promise. I think on the contrary that the rarity of the practice of compulsory voting is an indication of an obscure feeling that a compulsory requirement to vote is improper, even though one can argue in favour of it that, as with compulsory military service, it makes every citizen more fully aware of his responsibilities as a citizen. If participation in an election or a vote of any kind presupposes a promise, this would explain the general feeling that voting ought not to be compulsory.

What of the individual who chooses not to exercise his right to vote? Is it reasonable to impute to him an acceptance of the convention that the majority view shall be binding? Here I think we can only fall back again on the doctrine of consent. The man who abstains from voting has not given any promise; but if he does not actively protest against the whole business or try to leave the country, he may be assumed to acquiesce. The point is that the procedures of democratic government give him the opportunity of protesting and, if he can persuade enough people to agree with him, of changing the Government and the laws. If he lives under a system of government in which no genuine alternatives are made available to the electorate, I do not think we can attribute to him any willingly accepted obligation to obey a particular Government. Of course a citizen in such a State who thinks that the Government is pursuing the proper aims, will approve of the Government for that reason and will record his approval by a willing vote in its favour. But a citizen in such a State who records a vote in favour of the Government from fear, or who abstains, and who is prevented from leaving the country, cannot be said to have accepted the Government's authority or to be morally obliged.

Under a democratic system, does acceptance of governmental authority imply that it is never morally justifiable to refuse to obey a particular law? It is certainly justifiable, indeed it is part of the democratic process, to *campaign* against a law, i.e. to try to persuade a majority to agree with you and so to have the law changed. Is it also justifiable sometimes to *act* contrary to a law when you know that you are still in a minority? Yes, it may be. Political obligation does not exhaust the whole of our moral obligation, unless we take the view that the State is omnicompetent. There can be a conflict of moral obligations, and so there can be a conflict between political obligation and some other moral obligation. This is true, for example, of the conscientious objector who has failed to convince a tribunal, or of the supporter of nuclear disarmament who thinks he ought to protest in a forbidden area or to refuse to pay part of his taxes. Such a person, however, before deciding that he ought to disobey the law, needs to weigh up carefully the point and the extent of political obligation, reflecting that the State does in a large measure secure justice and essential interests as nothing else could. But if he considers that his conflicting obligation (e.g. to refrain from taking human life) is absolute or is otherwise clearly paramount, he is morally justified in disobedience. At the same time, if he agrees that in general his State attempts to secure justice and essential interests, and is therefore to be supported, he may conclude that he is morally obliged to accept whatever penalties the State decrees for disobedience. That is why I said in Chapter III, Section 2, that a conscientious objector may think he ought not to perform military service but that he ought to accept without protest the penalty of imprisonment. The same thing would apply to a supporter of nuclear disarmament who refuses, on conscientious grounds, to pay part of his taxes or who attends a protest meeting in a forbidden area.

My conclusion is that the grounds of political obligation in general depend on the moral ends or objectives of the State (with the proviso that consent must be added to give the State its authority). One is morally obliged to obey the law because one has a moral obligation to promote justice and the common good, and because State action is an essential means to the pursuit of those ends. When one disapproves of a particular Government or a particular law, one is nevertheless obliged, in a democratic society, to conform, if the policy followed has the assent of the majority; and one is then obliged because participation in the democratic procedure of election implies a promise to accept majority decisions. The convention of accepting majority decisions is followed because it is the only practicable approach to the ideal of universally agreed policies. Thus there is some truth in each of the theories I have considered, and that is why each of them still retains philosophical interest. But I should say that the theories of justice and the common good, when combined with the theory of consent, give the correct account of the grounds of political obligation in general.

V LIBERTY AND AUTHORITY

1 THE IDEA OF FREEDOM

'Freedom' means the absence of restraint. A man is free in so far as he is not restrained from doing what he wants to do or what he would choose to do if he knew that he could. The idea of choice itself implies a kind of freedom. Choice is the selection of one possibility among others. More than one possibility must be open to us before we can be said to have a choice. If we were always bound to do the one thing that we in fact do, we should not be free to choose; there would be no freedom of the will. The concept that I wish to discuss, however, is not the freedom of the will or freedom of choice, but the freedom to carry out what one has chosen to do. This is what is commonly meant by freedom or liberty in social and political discussion.

Having distinguished freedom of choice from freedom of action or social freedom, we may define the latter as the absence of restraint on doing what one chooses or what one would choose to do if he knew that he could. We must add, however, that the restraint must either be due to the deliberate action of other persons or be removable by the deliberate action of other persons. A man who is locked up in prison is not at liberty, because he is restrained by the action of other persons. And we may speak of freedom from want, or of freeing mankind from the scourge of cancer, when we mean that the impediments to which we refer, although not imposed by human action, are capable (we hope) of being removed by human action. But we should not say that a man is unfree because he is restrained by a natural impediment which cannot be removed by human action. If I do not have the natural physique to run a four-minute mile, we should say that I am 'unable', but not that I am 'not free', to do so.

The definition that I have given is, of course, a very general one. When freedom is mentioned in any particular context, it is always relevant to ask two questions: freedom from what? and freedom to do what? The first question asks what sort of restraint is to be removed or prevented. The second question asks what sort of actions are to be unrestrained. During the Second World War President Roosevelt and Mr. Churchill drew up, in the Atlantic Charter, a declaration of 'Four Freedoms' as their war aims. The four freedoms were: freedom of speech, freedom of worship, freedom from fear, freedom from want. You will notice that two of these are freedoms 'of' and two are freedoms 'from'. The first pair of freedoms specify two kinds of action which should be free or unrestrained; they answer the question, freedom to do what? 'Freedom of speech' is freedom to say what one likes. 'Freedom of worship' is freedom to practise whatever religion one chooses. The second pair of freedoms in the Atlantic Charter specify two kinds of restraint which should be removed or prevented; they answer the question, freedom from what? 'Freedom from fear' claims that men should not be prevented by fear from doing whatever they choose to do, fear of a Government with secret police such as the Nazis used, or fear of war and insecurity. 'Freedom from want' claims that men should not be prevented by want from doing what they would choose to do, want or poverty due to unemployment, the lack of a living wage, or the inability to work because of sickness or old age.

Two further features of the definition should be noted, since they are relevant to certain traditional criticisms of the common-sense concept of freedom. (1) In the first place, the definition is a negative one. It describes freedom as a negative concept, as the *absence* of restraint on doing what one chooses. (2) Secondly, something needs to be said about the word 'chooses' in the definition. Usually, what we *choose* to do is what we *want* to do. Sometimes it is not. Sometimes a man will choose to do one thing although he would like to do something else instead. In such a case he chooses the one action because he thinks it is the right thing to do. For example, he may choose to stand out for an unpopular cause, which he believes to be right, although it would be easier and more comfortable for him to go along with the majority. He chooses to follow his conscience rather than his inclination. In these circumstances freedom to do as we choose is freedom of conscience. But more often, as I have said, what a man chooses to do is what he wants to do; and then freedom to do as we choose is freedom to do as we wish. Doing what we want to do may happen to coincide with doing what we think right, or it may go against what we think right, or it may be quite irrelevant to questions of conscience. The main point is that doing what we choose to do is usually doing what we want to do, so that freedom, as I have defined it, is most often a matter of being unrestrained in doing what one wants.

The definition of freedom that I have given is fairly simple, and I think that it, or something like it, is obviously what we normally mean by the term. This common-sense concept of freedom, however, has been criticized by a long line of philosophers on two grounds connected with the two points that I have just noted.

(1) First, objection has been taken to the negative character of the common-sense notion of freedom. Freedom, it is said, is too precious a thing to be merely negative. Freedom is one of the highest values of human life, and therefore it must be something vital and positive. This criticism has come mainly from philosophical Idealists, in the technical sense of that term. Philosophical Idealism is a metaphysical doctrine which holds that the mental or spiritual is real and the material is not. It is called 'Idealism' because it regards 'ideas', the contents and activities of minds, as the stuff of reality. This metaphysical doctrine is not directly relevant to social and political theory. But it so happens that the most influential school of philosophical Idealists has also held the ethical theory of Self-Realization, the theory that the end of human life is to realize the 'true' or 'higher' self. Since these philosophers think that self-realization is the ultimate

value, they have argued that freedom must have a close connection with self-realization if freedom is to be a value. A man is
truly free, they have argued, when he has realized his true self.
Freedom is to be defined in terms of self-realization, which is a
positive notion, not a mere negative one.

I do not think that this objection to our common-sense definition of freedom need worry us. All that it comes to is this: if
freedom is a negative concept, then freedom cannot be the
ultimate value. That consequence can be accepted. Whether
or not we agree that the ultimate value is self-realization, our
common-sense definition of freedom does imply that self-
realization or self-development has *a* value. If we attach importance to freedom, understood as I have defined it, this means
that we think it important that a man should not be restrained
from giving effect to his choices. We can think that important
only if we attach value to choice and the exercise of choice.
Liberty is a necessary condition of self-development or self-
fulfilment and is valued as a means to self-fulfilment. This does
not mean, however, that self-development or self-fulfilment is
the *same* as liberty. Nor does it imply that freedom is of little
account because it is only a means to an end. The fact that
something is a means to an end, and not an end in itself, does
not make it of comparatively small importance. If it is a *necessary* means to a vital value, then it is itself vital.

(2) The common-sense concept of freedom is also criticized on
the ground that it makes freedom a means to doing what we
want; the end which it serves is 'mere desire'. But, the argument
proceeds, there is nothing of value in mere desire. The kind of
action that has value is moral action, the doing of what is good
or right. An individual's desires often go against this. Freedom
to do as one likes is not liberty but licence. This second criticism
is a very old one, and goes right back to Plato and Aristotle. But,
like the first criticism, it is also common in the work of the
philosophical Idealists and is tied up with their notion of self-
realization.

I have in fact defined freedom in terms of choice, and not
simply in terms of what a man wants or desires to do. But I have

agreed that usually it *is* a matter of desire. Desires may be bad
and they may be good. What makes a bad desire bad? I suggest
it is the fact that the desire in question is hostile to other desires,
of the agent or of other persons. The satisfaction of any desire,
considered simply as a satisfaction or pleasure, is to that extent
good, and a right action would not be right unless, among other
conditions, it was intended to promote someone's interest, i.e.
to satisfy desires whether in the short or the long run. When the
satisfaction of a particular desire is thought bad or wrong, this
is because it thwarts the satisfaction of other actual or potential
desires, in the agent or in others, which are regarded, for one
reason or another, as more important than the first desire. The
goodness and badness of desires is carried over to the means of
satisfying them. If the satisfaction of any desire, considered
simply as a satisfaction, has some degree of goodness, so has the
freedom to obtain that satisfaction. But if the satisfying of a
particular desire thwarts the satisfaction of others, the thwarting
is a restriction of freedom, so that freedom to satisfy the one
desire involves a lack of freedom to satisfy the others. 'Licence',
or freedom that is disapproved, is freedom of this kind. Considered
simply as an instance of freedom it has an initial claim to be
considered good, but if the freedom that it restricts has a stronger
claim, then its badness as a cause of unfreedom outweighs its
goodness as being an instance of freedom itself.

   In the light of their two criticisms of the common-sense
concept of freedom, Idealists have been led to identify 'true'
freedom with the doing of one's duty. This is positive and always
good. Occasionally, to be sure, a duty is felt to be a form of
restraint on doing what we should like, but this, according to
the Idealist, does not mean that we are unfree in doing our duty.
For when we perform a duty we exercise freedom of choice (or
free will), which is the true form of freedom. The freedom to
do as we like, which may be restrained by the requirements
of duty, is not a true or real freedom. Indeed, a man who feels
the call of duty as a restraint is already in bondage to his desires,
his 'lower self'. He has not fully realized the 'higher self', in
which perfect freedom is to be found.

This line of argument fails to make the necessary distinction between freedom of choice and freedom to give effect to one's choices. It also confuses freedom of choice with what may be called the 'freedom of inner harmony'. When a man finds that the following of duty involves no tension with his desires, he has reached a harmony between conscience and desire. Since there is no conflict between them, neither is felt as a restraint upon the other, and the following of either motive is free from internal restraint. Such a freedom of inner harmony, when perfectly developed, may be a form of necessity, in the sense that the agent has no choice; he necessarily does what conscience and desire alike move him to do. He is not restrained, but he also has no choice. A saint (or, in the language of Immanuel Kant, a person with a 'holy will') would have this character. It is proper to say that he would exercise a form of perfect freedom, and religious doctrine so describes it. But it differs from freedom of choice, for the 'holy will' necessarily follows one path while freedom of choice is freedom to adopt either of two (or more) possibilities. Freedom of moral choice is freedom to choose either right *or wrong*. A free choice of what is wrong is no less free, in this sense of 'free', than is a free choice of what is right.

The Idealist, therefore, reaches his view of 'true' freedom by confusing together three different things, freedom of inner harmony, freedom of choice, and freedom to give effect to our choices. The saint who necessarily does what is right possesses the freedom of inner harmony but does not have freedom of choice. The man who has freedom of choice may exercise that freedom in choosing what is wrong as well as in choosing what is right. If he also possesses the social freedom of not being restrained from giving effect to his choice, this social freedom may be bad (when he does what is wrong and harmful to others) just as easily as it may be good. The freedom of inner harmony may be called 'perfect' in that its exercise is never bad. It is not what is meant by the word 'freedom' when used in social and political contexts. Social freedom is not always and unreservedly a good thing; some restraints upon it are essential. The fact that we usually think it good should not mislead us into supposing that it is always so and thereby into confusing it with a different form of freedom which is relevant to ethics and religion but not to politics.

Although the idealist concept of freedom confuses different senses of the term, it does have a point in directing our attention to the potentialities of human nature rather than to actual present desires. There are circumstances in which a man's present desires do not form the determining factor for saying whether or not he enjoys freedom. Consider the example of a slave who is contented with his lot and genuinely does not want any different status. If freedom is defined as the absence of restraint on satisfying present desires, it follows that the contented slave is not unfree. A discontented slave who wants to be released from his present state is unfree, because the legal conditions of his status are a restraint upon his wishes. The contented slave is subject to the same legal conditions, but they are not a restraint upon his wishes since he does not want to change his situation. Or take the example of someone who has been 'brain-washed' into acceptance of a repressive political régime, like Winston Smith in George Orwell's novel *Nineteen Eighty-Four*. Before he was brain-washed, Winston Smith certainly felt unfree. By the time the manipulators have finished with him, he loves Big Brother and does not want things to be any different. We need to remember that there are two ways in which a man may be rid of an obstacle to the satisfaction of a desire. The obvious way is for the obstacle to be removed, so that the desire may be fulfilled. The less obvious way is for the man to stop, or to be made to stop, desiring what he cannot attain. If he no longer has the desire, it may be said that the lack of freedom which was presented by the obstacle no longer exists. The obstacle itself remains, but it is no longer, for him, an obstacle to the satisfaction of desire. He is content to be as he is, and therefore he has what he wants. Yet we should not be inclined to say of a contented slave, or of a brain-washed Winston Smith, that he ceases to be unfree just because his present desires are not restrained by his legal or political situation. In thinking of freedom we assume a norm of human nature in which the desire for self-fulfilment *would* be restrained by the conditions of slavery or of the political régime of *Nineteen Eighty-Four*. We assume (and, I think, on good evidence) that if the contented slave were given a taste of emancipation and were then asked to choose between it and his former status, he would prefer emancipation. Although some slaves are contented with their lot if they are well treated, and although some emancipated slaves may at first feel overwhelmed by the responsibility of having to fend for themselves, one would have to go far to find a slave who would choose to remain in slavery if offered his freedom, and farther still to find one who, having been emancipated, would choose to return to slavery, preferring the fleshpots of Egypt to the hardships of Sinai. Likewise we are certainly justified in contrasting natural choice with the submission induced by brain-washing or similar techniques, and prisoners-of-war who have been subjected to such treatment soon revert to a normal frame of mind after their release from the prison camp.

The definition of freedom which I have given is intended to allow for what I have just called a norm of human nature. I have defined freedom as the absence of restraint on doing what one chooses or what one would choose to do if he knew that he could. Our 'norm of human nature', when we think of freedom, is not a visionary ideal to be attained only by exceptional persons; it is the human nature that we attribute to normal human beings. A slave has been, in a sense, dehumanized: 'Zeus takes away half the virtue of a man when the day of slavery comes upon him'.[1] Still more obviously is this true of brain-washing. The norm of natural choices and desires that we take as standard in our concept of freedom is not a 'higher' or 'best' self, as the Idealists suggest, but the natural character of an average human being in normal circumstances.

2 LIBERTY AND LAW

I argued in Chapter IV that if the State is to be regarded as authoritative, there must be moral grounds for political obligation.

---

[1] Homer, *Odyssey*, XVII. 322–3.

Such grounds, I suggested, may be found in the ends pursued by the State. If the State aims at the moral ends of justice and the common good, our independent moral obligation to pursue these ends implies an obligation to accept a necessary means to them. The means in question is the legal apparatus of the State.

State action, that is, the use of law and its sanctions, is applied, in a democratic society, only where the relevant moral ends cannot be adequately secured without it. Law restricts liberty in requiring us to do things that we might otherwise not want to do, and in requiring us to refrain from actions that we might otherwise want to do. The restrictions upon liberty imposed by the law may be intended to protect the liberty of others (or sometimes of oneself) which would be impeded by the behaviour that the law restricts, or alternatively the restrictions of law may be intended to promote other values than liberty (though, as we shall see, it is often possible to regard those values as including the promotion of liberty in some respects). For either of these reasons the restrictions of law may be desirable, indeed essential. Nevertheless they are restrictions upon liberty, and therefore a democratic society, which sets a high value on maintaining a maximum of liberty, deliberately limits the scope of State authority. Just where the limits should be placed, however, is a matter of controversy. There is considerable difference of opinion, not just about details of application, but even about the general principles that should mark the boundary between the scope of law and that of individual freedom. We may illustrate the difficulties in four fields of State action.

(a) Crime

The prevention of much harmful action, of a minor kind, is left to agencies other than the State. It is left to the instruction of the family or religious institutions or schools, and to the influence exerted by public opinion. The force of law is brought in only where a type of socially harmful action is felt to be *seriously* harmful to society (e.g. murder, theft), or is likely to be *widespread* without the sanction of State action (e.g. parking a motor car in such a way as to be a nuisance or a danger). Such action is what is meant by a criminal offence and is dealt with by that branch of the law which is called the criminal law. People sometimes talk of a distinction between crime and sin. But since the concept of sin is a religious one, meaning a wilful breach of divine command, and since many people nowadays would not be prepared to give morality a religious interpretation, it is more appropriate, for the purposes of social discussion, to speak of a distinction between crime and moral wrongdoing. Not all wrongful action is forbidden by law and so regarded as crime. Generally speaking, wrongful action is made subject to criminal law only if it meets one of the two conditions that I have specified, namely, either if it is *seriously* harmful to society, or if it is likely to cause *widespread* social harm when left without legal control even though the *degree* of harm in any particular instance may not be very great. Thus we have laws against nuisance as well as against murder and theft.

If this criterion were always strictly applied, it would follow that action which is harmful only to the individual agent himself should not be made the subject of law, i.e. should not be regarded as crime. This position is strongly advocated by John Stuart Mill in his essay *On Liberty*, a classic document of liberal-democratic thought. According to this view, if a man chooses to drink himself silly in his own home, so long as he does not make himself a nuisance to others, and so long as his behaviour does not bring any harm upon others, such as his dependants, then it is his own business and not the business of the State. We may deplore the fact that he is allowing himself to become morally degraded, but we should not use the sanctions of the criminal law to prevent it. Other examples would be drug-taking (which is in fact subject to legal control in most countries) and suicide or attempted suicide (which were regarded as crimes in English Law until quite recently).

Of course many people would disagree with Mill's position. Objection may be taken to it on either of two grounds. (1) It may be argued that no action is without social effects. For example, very few drunkards will be adversely affecting no-one other than themselves; most will have wives and families who will suffer from their squandering their money and from their brutishness; in the other cases, there is at least the harmful influence of example. This objection is not to the principle of Mill's position, but to its unreality, its lack of application. (2) Other people, however, may object to the principle itself, arguing that the State ought to be concerned with the moral welfare of the individual agent.

Here is one respect in which there can be difference of opinion about the limits to be set to the functions of the State. The argument concerns the limits of State authority and those of individual liberty. How far should a man be left free to do as he chooses with regard to his own life?

(b) Civil disputes

Civil law deals with disputes between individuals or corporate bodies. In so far as the civil law concerns wrongs, they are wrongs which are not treated as crimes, i.e. as deliberate harm to the fabric of the organized society itself. They are acts which have caused harm to individuals, e.g. because of negligence, and for which a man is held liable to pay damages but not liable to punishment. There can also be disputes as to who has the right on his side, e.g. in actions for alleged wrongful dismissal, breach of contract, divorce, and so on. Here the apparatus of the State is brought in to arbitrate on a dispute. It is not clear where the rights and wrongs lie, and somebody has to decide.

Many disputes of this kind must be decided by the State because the principles at stake are basic to the ordering of society, and indeed a breach of these principles may at times impinge on matters that are subject to the criminal law. For example, some breaches of contract, if deliberate, may involve or come near to such crimes as fraud. Some cases of negligence (e.g. in driving a motor car) may be so serious as to warrant a criminal charge, and in consequence the criminal law does not always insist on the doctrine of *mens rea*, the doctrine that wrongful action cannot be criminal unless it is done with deliberate intention.

Not all civil disputes which require arbitration, however, need be referred to the courts of law. I do not mean simply that disputes can be settled 'out of court' by lawyers who have a good idea of what a court would do if called upon to decide. I mean that the parties to a dispute may agree to accept the verdict of an arbitrator who has nothing to do with the State and its courts of law. For example, an insurance policy may say that in some circumstances a disagreement about liability shall be referred to an independent assessor for adjudication. No doubt one of the reasons for preferring the voluntary procedure is that it costs less than recourse to the courts; but this is not the only reason. Compulsory arbitration need not mean arbitration by ordinary courts of law and need not be as costly. If it were thought necessary, insurance companies could be required by statute to submit disagreements to a special arbitration tribunal, the operation of which could be as inexpensive and as speedy as a voluntary procedure. The reason why this is not done is that it is unnecessary. In a democratic society, voluntary methods are preferred to State intervention so long as the subject of dispute is one that can be settled by voluntary methods with justice and stability.

On the one hand, then, there are disputes that clearly must be decided by the courts or other agencies of the State, and on the other hand there are disputes that clearly do not need State intervention. Between the two groups there is an area of uncertainty, an area of disputes or disagreements which some people will regard as calling for State intervention while others will not. I shall give two examples.

One obvious example is furnished by some industrial disputes. The general question how far the State should exercise control over employers and workers in wage-bargaining is more appropriate for my next sub-heading, economic control, than for the present one of disputes under civil law. Issues of civil law do arise, however, when strike action is in breach of a contract of employment. Some people think that such strikes should be made illegal, others that this would be an unwarranted interference with the freedom of workers to obtain improved conditions for themselves. The one side argues in favour of State intervention in order to protect the rights of contract in the interests of justice and the common good. The other side argues against State intervention on the ground that it would limit essential liberties of individuals and of social groups such as Trade Unions.

My second example concerns the liberty of the press, in relation to the general interest or to the liberty of individuals. In 1953 the proprietors and editors of newspapers in Britain set up a voluntary Press Council to consider complaints of improper conduct. The freedom of the press is of course restricted by law to some extent, for instance in regard to libel. But many things appear in the newspapers which, while not illegal, may be thought to overstep the bounds of a proper decency; for example, intrusion into the private lives of people who happen to be connected with some event, perhaps a tragic one, that has come into the news. The decisions of the Press Council on complaints brought before it are recommendations only, and some people think it is insufficiently effective. It could be given statutory recognition, like the General Medical Council, so that its decisions would have to be followed on pain of legal sanctions. Those who would like to strengthen the hand of the Press Council may say that this is required in the public interest or in order to safeguard some of the rights or freedoms of the individual private person. On the other hand, it can be argued that a maximum of freedom for the press is itself, despite possible abuses, a bulwark for the protection of the public interest. Here again, then, there is room for difference of opinion about the limits of State authority.

(c) Economic control

I have already mentioned wage-bargaining as a feature of economic life which may or may not be subject to State control. Of course the very idea of wage-bargaining only applies where there is a free market economy. Under a communist régime wages are fixed by governmental agency; there is no bargaining between employers and workers, and no threat of strike on the one side or of declaring redundancies on the other. Where there is a system of wage-bargaining, one cannot expect that solutions to disputes will be reached by sweet reason alone. Employers and workers will not usually agree on what a firm or industry can afford, or on what would be a just division of earnings into wages and profits. It therefore seems to be inevitable that the workers must retain a right to strike and the employers a right of dismissal. Yet it does not need to be an absolute right in either case. The indiscriminate use of the right to strike can be so harmful to the community at large that some measure of State control seems justifiable. How far State intervention should go, however, is a matter on which there will be many different opinions. Drawing a line between a completely free economy and a completely controlled one is an excessively ticklish business.

Industrial relations are of course not the only aspect of economic life in which this problem arises. The nineteenth-century Utilitarians held that the State ought not to interfere at all in the economic life of the nation, and especially that there should be complete freedom for manufacturers and traders: *laissez-faire*, *laissez-passer*. They took the view that a completely free market led to the greatest contribution to the general interest. To-day few people would be so confident about the benefits of a completely free economy, and everyone would agree that *some* part of the economy must be subject to public control. Atomic energy, for instance, is too dangerous to be left in private hands. In regard to other industries and services there is difference of opinion whether public control or private enterprise contributes most to the general interest. Socialists tend to think that the public interest is best served by the nationalization of basic industries and services; conservatives think that efficiency, and so the best contribution to the public interest, depends on the incentives of profit and competition.

In some matters, questions of justice to particular interests, rather than contributions to the general interest, may afford a ground for State intervention. An example is the provision of air services to the Scottish Highlands and Islands, or of rail services in sparsely populated areas. These services cannot pay their way; but in order that the inhabitants of those areas should have a reasonable share of the speedy transport facilities that are available to people in other parts of the country, the Government may require air lines and railways to provide services.

Similarly, manufacturers may be induced by the State to build new factories in areas where there is chronic unemployment, although it might be more economical, from the point of view of the manufacturers at least, to add to their existing factories elsewhere. Consider again the system of taxation. A heavily graduated scheme of taxation and of death duties, which 'soaks the rich', curtails the possibilities of amassing private property. It may thereby reduce incentives and so result in a lower total national product than would otherwise be realized. The reason for such measures is a conception of justice or fairness. There will be differences of opinion on the extent to which this idea of fairness should be held to outweigh liberty and scope for initiative. In the Britain of to-day, the Conservative and Labour Parties both agree that some weight should be given to incentive for the sake of individual freedom and of a high total national product, and that some weight should be given to the reduction of inequality for the sake of social justice; but conservatives tilt the balance more in favour of the former, while socialists tilt it more towards the latter.

All governmental action in the field of economics restricts the liberty of some people. They are not allowed to do just as they please. If some types of strike are made illegal, workers have less freedom of action in the tactics of wage-bargaining. If the iron and steel industry is nationalized, the owners of foundries and steel mills are no longer free to conduct their businesses as they wish for their own profit. They must sell out and either betake themselves to a different form of business or else, if they choose to remain as managers, they must accept orders from a State-appointed Board and work for a fixed salary. The air line that is required to provide uneconomical services to sparsely populated areas as a condition of being allowed to continue with other services, is not given the freedom that it would like to make as large a profit as possible. And everyone who is required to pay taxes, large or small, is not free to spend that money as he would like to do. Governmental restrictions on economic freedom are imposed for the sake of the general moral objectives of the common good and justice; and while everyone nowadays would accept the necessity of some governmental intervention in the economic sphere, there is disagreement on the extent to which the moral ends of the State justify the curtailment of individual liberty. Often, on economic matters, the disagreement is about means, on whether public control, e.g. of the iron and steel industry, will in fact serve the general interest better than private enterprise would. But at times, as in the system of taxation, it is disagreement about ends, about the comparative weight to be given to one moral objective as against another.

(d) Provision of social welfare

In most modern advanced societies, the State provides a subsistence benefit to meet basic needs when a person cannot earn his living owing to unemployment or old age or illness. There may be, in addition, State provision for medical care. Some of these matters are controversial. But every civilized nation regards it as a responsibility of the State to provide educational services, at least at the elementary level, and although this is not usually regarded as an aspect of the 'Welfare State' it is in fact the same sort of thing, meeting a basic social need. The provision of social welfare in some degree is acknowledged by all to be a proper function of the State.

As with other forms of State action, the laws that give effect to this function restrict individual liberty. They obviously do so in their financial requirements. Social security schemes and educational services have to be paid for, by way of social insurance contributions and general taxation, and, as I said a little earlier, the legal requirement to give up a proportion of one's income to the State means that one is not free to do as one likes with the money. Other restrictions on freedom are involved too. For example, the State may make it compulsory for parents to have their children educated, or, in order to prevent epidemics, it may require everyone to be immunized against certain infectious diseases. The degree of compulsion can vary. While making it compulsory for every child to be educated up to the age of, say, 15 or 16, a State may leave parents free to choose between public and private education. Vaccination soon after birth used to be compulsory in Britain; now it is only recommended, but if an epidemic of smallpox were to break out in a particular area the people living there might be required to undergo vaccination.

Some of these restrictions on liberty are made for the sake of the common good, others for the sake of justice. Educational and health services are established partly for the sake of the general interest; an educated and skilled citizen is more useful to the community than an ignorant one, and a fit worker is more useful than a sick one. The same sort of thing may perhaps be said of unemployment benefit. But it cannot be said of old-age pensions. A person who is too old to work cannot make a return to the community for the benefit he receives. Justice, not the general interest, is the ground here. It is felt that the community owes it to everyone, as a moral right, that he should not be left to starve in old age. Similar considerations of justice, or human rights, in fact come into the other provisions also. When we judge that everyone ought to be given a reasonable education, the services of doctors and hospitals when needed, and the means of subsistence in times of sickness or unemployment, we are surely thinking of what is due to them as individuals and not simply of the potential benefit to society.

In the field of social welfare, as in the other fields of State action, there is difference of opinion about the extent to which the State should make legal requirements, thereby restricting liberty, for the sake of its general moral objectives of justice and the common good. Some people think that there should be ample scope for a choice of private education or privately-paid medical services alongside the public system. Others think that the inequality of treatment which this allows as between the rich and the poor is an offence to social justice. Some think that social security should be cut to a minimum, lest they sap initiative and encourage sponging on the State; others think that it is better to run these risks than to permit hardship.

When the State restricts liberty, it can often be said to do so in order to enhance liberty in other respects. I have spoken of the moral objectives of the State as the promotion of justice and the common good. 'Justice' here includes the old function of protecting established rights as well as the newer function of making a more fair distribution of rights, and since a man's rights can often be regarded as freedoms the protection or granting of a right is often a protection or granting of freedom. For example, when the criminal law restricts freedom to take other people's goods, in protecting security it protects freedom, since theft is a restraint on the freedom of the property owner to make use of his property as he wishes. Again, a redistribution of rights, whether in terms of opportunities, as in education, or in terms of income, as in a scheme of social security, reduces the freedom of some people to do as they would like and increases the similar freedom of others. The same goes for the objective of the common good or general interest. The general interest means the interest of most members of the community, and a policy which advances the interest of most people is one that gives them more scope for doing as they would like to do. So that while law restricts liberty, it is also true to say that a decent measure of liberty for all can only be secured within the framework of a system of law. Nevertheless the fact that one kind of liberty can conflict with another, or that more liberty for some people means less for others, often raises difficulty and dispute in determining the proper limits of State action.

3   THE LIMITS OF STATE AUTHORITY

We are thus brought back to a question that was raised by implication in Chapter II, Section 5(c), where I discussed the State's functions and referred to the opposed ideas of the omnicompetent and of the minimal State. Can one lay down any general principles about the proper limits of State authority? The examples that I have given of disagreement on issues in the different fields of State action show that one cannot hope to find a clear-cut answer. It would be a foolish philosophy which rushed in where practice treads delicately. A man's view on these disputed matters will depend on his general political and moral outlook, and that cannot be determined by philosophy alone.

One thing that philosophy can do, however, is to show, by its clarification of concepts, that *some* limits on State action are necessary and that the idea of the omnicompetent State often neglects certain essential distinctions. From a practical point of view this may seem a trivial task, since few people, in liberal democracies at least, would want to advocate omnicompetence for the State. Yet the idea of omnicompetence has had its attractions even for thinkers of a democratic cast of mind, and it is important to expose theoretical errors that are liable to recur. There is a strong temptation for political philosophy to suppose that it can give positive guidance for practice, and the influence of attempts to do so is far from negligible. If one thinks that these attempts are misguided, the remedy is to show them up and not just to desist from further attempts oneself.

I wrote in Chapter II, Section 5(c), that to say the State is omnicompetent may mean either of three things: that the State may, or that it does, or that it should, undertake any and every possible function. I added that, in practice, no State does, and I reserved for further consideration the views that it may or that it should. I deal first with the idea that it *may*.

If we think, not only of totalitarian States, but of a democratic State like Britain that does not have a fixed constitution, we are inclined to say that the powers of the State are unlimited. This is not true of a country which has a fixed constitution setting limits to what may be done. Such a constitution, however, usually contains provision for its own amendment. If amendment without limits can be carried out by legislative process, then the State may be said to have unlimited powers after all; what is limited is the power of a particular branch or arm of the State. In Britain, however, it would seem that one arm of the State, the legislature, has unlimited powers. It has been said: 'Parliament can do anything except turn a man into a woman'. In one sense it is false to add the exception; in another sense it is false to make the general statement, 'Parliament can do anything', unless this is qualified by exceptions of a more radical character. We need to recall the two senses of the word 'can' which I distinguished in Chapter III, Section 4. If we are thinking of legal possibilities, of what Parliament *may* do, then Parliament is indeed omnicompetent, and there is no need to add any exceptions at all. But if we are thinking of practical possibilities, of laws that Parliament can make effectively, the exceptions are far wider than the old tag suggests. If Parliament were so foolish as to pass a Bill providing that, as from a specified date, a certain John Jones shall be deemed to be a woman, this would not contravene any rule of constitutional law and so would not exceed Parliament's legal powers; but it would be thought crazy, and neither the comic Act nor the Parliament which made it would retain any respect. As I said in Chapter III, Section 4, legal 'bonds' and 'powers' or 'facilities' are fictions, not natural facts. But if they are to be effective, they must be of such a kind that most people will choose to act as if they were facts. If they fly too flagrantly in the face of facts, and especially in the face of the psychological facts of what people are prepared to put up with, they will have no force. There are no legal limitations on what Parliament *may* enact; there are substantial practical limitations on what it *can* enact effectively.

The practical limitations do not depend only on the natural facts of physics or biology, as is suggested by the statement that Parliament can do anything except turn a man into a woman. They depend also, and indeed more, on the natural facts of psychology. In *Alice in Wonderland*, the King of Hearts tries to get rid of Alice at the trial of the Knave by inventing the rule, 'All persons more than a mile high to leave the court'. Suppose a Parliament consisting of self-consciously small men were to pass a Bill stating that all persons more than five feet ten inches in height should be executed. This would be a valid law, and there would be no physical or biological impossibility in trying to put it into effect. But it would be psychologically impossible. If such a Bill were passed by the Parliament, there would be a revolution. On the other hand, if a majority of the populace shares the views of the legislature on a measure, it can sometimes be given effect even if it flies in the face of some biological facts, e.g. if laws concerning racial discrimination presuppose that different 'races' have different brain structures.

Even in a totalitarian régime there are some things which people will not stand for. No State has unlimited practical or political power to make any law that it pleases, even though it may possess unlimited legal power. A legislature that has any sense and that wants to remain in office will pay more regard to political than to legal possibilities, to what it can effectively do than to what it may legally do.

I turn now to the remaining sense of the doctrine of omnicompetence, namely that the State *should* undertake all the functions that it can perform. The word 'can' here needs to be understood as meaning 'effectively can' and not as meaning 'may'. If I am not able to do something, there is no sense in considering whether I ought to. The fact that there is no legal bar is irrelevant. So it would be pointless to ask whether the State ought to do everything that it may do. The question that matters is whether it ought to undertake all the functions that it can, practically or politically, perform.

The advocate of State omnicompetence in this sense can put his position very simply in the first instance. The State exists 'for the sake of the good life', as Aristotle said. It exists in order to forward moral objectives, justice and the common good. Therefore it ought to do everything possible to forward those objectives.

On the other hand it can be argued, again in moral terms, that State action inhibits the morally good life. The methods used by the State are those of compulsion, law backed by sanctions. The point of bringing in State action to secure some aim is that this aim would not be followed by all unless some were compelled. Now compulsion is morally objectionable, because it is of the essence of moral action that it should be freely chosen. Hence, the argument proceeds, the use of legal compulsion to secure moral aims destroys the possibility of acting from a moral motive. So that if the State tries to make itself responsible for the good life, the life so produced ceases to be the morally good life. The argument can be summarized as saying that legal compulsion inhibits the exercise of moral freedom, the free choice of right action for moral reasons.

This objection can, however, be carried too far. If the law requires or forbids some kind of action, this does not imply that *everyone* is going to conform under compulsion, instead of from moral motives. Bill Sykes refrains from burgling only because he sees the policeman on his beat and is afraid of being caught and imprisoned. But most people refrain from burgling because they think it would be wrong anyway. As we have seen in Chapter III, Section 3, the authority of the law, although it does depend on and make use of sanctions, could not be effective unless most people accepted it on moral grounds. If most people recognize a moral obligation to obey the law, they are acting from a moral motive and not under compulsion.

The objection that State action inhibits moral freedom, a form of freedom of choice, is therefore not a particularly strong one. A more telling objection is the obvious one that legal compulsion restricts social freedom, freedom of action. This is also a value, an essential part of 'the good life'; and if State action restricts social freedom more than it need, then the State diminishes the good life.

As against this, of course, it may be replied that freedom is not the only constituent of the good life and that the value of freedom may have to be sacrificed for the sake of a greater or more fundamental value. But this reply will not suffice to defend the doctrine of State omnicompetence. For it allows that freedom is one value among others, and therefore it must admit the possibility that at times the value of freedom may outweigh competing values such as security. The authority of the State will need to be limited by this possibility.

Most political theorists recognize that individual liberty and State authority conflict with each other, and that a balance has to be struck between them and the values they represent. Some, like Hobbes, are prepared to say that liberty must be severely limited to make way for the benefits of State authority. Others, like Locke and J. S. Mill, think that State authority should be markedly limited so as to leave as much room as possible for liberty. Both Hobbes on the one side, and Locke and Mill on the other, agree that liberty and authority can conflict; it is not possible for complete liberty and complete authority to exist together. There is, however, a line of thought which tries to say that the two do go together and that omnicompetence for the State is the only way to secure full and genuine freedom. The arguments used for this conclusion are derived from Plato, developed in Rousseau's theory of the general will, and continued by the idealist philosophers to whom I referred in Section 1 of this chapter. The conclusion reached is the paradoxical one that compulsion by the State can make a man more free, not less, that in fact a man who is constrained by the law for the sake of moral ends can be, in Rousseau's phrase, 'forced to be free'.[1]

This extraordinary view depends on the Idealist's interpretation of 'true' freedom as the performance of one's duty. Freedom of choice may be exercised in situations of moral conflict, i.e. conflict between what is morally right and what one desires to do. Now sometimes, when a man is carried away by desires, we speak of his being a slave to his desires. If this happens in a situation of moral conflict, the agent does not have freedom of choice. Because of this, some theorists, from Plato onwards, have held that *any* action motivated by desire is not freely chosen but is determined. By contrast, they have argued, action which is motivated by the sense of duty is rational (reason being contrasted with desire) and free. Thus they have reached the view that the only kind of free action is morally right action. A man who 'chooses' to follow his desires, against his sense of duty, is not acting freely; a man who does what he likes or wants, irrespective of whether it is in conflict with duty or not, is not acting freely. It is action determined or compelled by desire. Only the doing of what is right is free, because it is rational. Add the view that what the State requires is right, and we can understand more clearly the theory of the general or 'real' will. The State's aim is the common good, and this is both what we ought to pursue and what we really want. So that we are really free, doing what we really want and acting rightly (the two are identical, it is claimed), when we pursue the common good. And if a particular individual wants to pursue some particular

[1] *Contrat social*, I. 7.

private interest of his own, this can only be his 'apparent' will. It is what he thinks he wants, not what he really wants. If he follows this apparent will, he thinks he is free, he thinks he is doing what he wants. But in reality he is not free, for he is not pursuing what he really wants, the common good. He is enslaved by desire for particular interest, instead of acting freely for the common interest. When the State compels him to act so as to serve the common good, it is compelling him to do what he really wants, and so compelling him to be free.

Some of the confusions inherent in this view will already be apparent from my discussion of the theory of the general will in Chapter IV, Section 5, and of the idealist theory of freedom in Section 1 of the present chapter. To these must be added a comment on the argument that motivation by desire is a form of bondage. I shall make that comment first and shall then add to it a repetition of the earlier objections.

(1) From the fact that we *sometimes* speak of a man as being a slave to his desires, the theory infers that motivation by desire is *always* a form of bondage. If this were a deductive argument, it would of course be fallacious; the proposition that some men have red noses (or that some desires enslave) does not imply that all men have red noses (or that all desires enslave). Presumably the argument is meant to depend on induction or analogy, and to yield a conclusion of probability only. But then our use of the language of enslavement or bondage in relation to desires is limited to a narrow range of actions, which appear to be discernibly different from others, and which therefore cannot be used as evidence for a generalization about all action motivated by desire. A man who is addicted to drugs or to smoking may know that he would *prefer* to get out of the habit but is unable to do so. He feels helpless, and certainly does not regard himself as being free to do as he wishes or chooses. Our experience is quite different in the case of an ordinary sort of desire, when we do an action because we prefer it. Both in our thought and in our language about such experience we presuppose that we exercise choice. The kleptomaniac feels that he is subject to a compulsive urge; the ordinary thief does not. That is why we can distinguish

between kleptomania and normal theft. Since action due to the
force of addiction or neurosis feels different from normal action,
the fact that the former may be described as enslavement to
desire does not justify us in saying that all action motivated by
desire is enslaved or unfree.

(2) The theory confuses freedom of choice with freedom of
action or social freedom. Enslavement by desire implies that
there is no freedom of choice. But when we speak of having or
not having liberty or freedom in a political context, we are
referring to freedom of action or social freedom, i.e. the absence
of restraint or compulsion by human agency, including compulsion by the State. No doubt compulsion by the State can prevent
compulsion by desire from being effective in action, as when the
law controls the sale of addictive drugs; but this is just sub-
stituting one form of unfreedom for another. It does not give the
drug addict freedom of choice (though it may be a necessary step
towards restoring freedom of choice in due course), and it certainly does not give him freedom of action.

(3) When discussing freedom of choice in situations of moral
conflict, the theory supposes that moral freedom applies only in
one direction, as the freedom to do what is right. But if moral
freedom did not allow of genuine alternatives, to do what is
right or not to do so, it would not be choice. The theory infers
that we can be forced to be free, because it equates 'being free'
with 'doing what is right'. The paradoxical conclusion simply
means that we can be forced to do what is right. This may well be
justifiable, but not on the ground that it gives us freedom. If
we are forced, we are not free. We do what is right, but not
freely.

(4) While a person may not always know what he wants,
usually he does; and when he does, there is no reason whatever
for saying that he is mistaken and that the State can know better
than he what he himself wants. What he wants to do may be
wrong, because harmful to others, or perhaps because harmful
to himself; and if so, it may be justifiable to restrain him by
legal compulsion, on the ground that what he wants to do is
wrong. But it cannot be justifiable on the ground that he is now

enslaved and that the legal compulsion will make him free. Compulsory freedom is a self-contradiction. Freedom is not the only value, and it is often justifiable to restrict a man's freedom for the sake of other values or for the sake of the freedom of other people. But if we do think it is justifiable, we should recognize that it is a restriction of freedom and to that extent bad.

The one positive conclusion that emerges from our criticism of the idea of the omnicompetent State is that there ought to be *some* limit to the exercise of State authority, simply because legal compulsion restricts freedom and freedom is desirable. Even the advocate of omnicompetence agrees that freedom is a value; that is why he tries to make out that State omnicompetence enhances freedom. On the other hand, freedom is not the only value, and therefore we cannot follow the doctrine of the minimal State in holding that the sole criterion for the bounds of State authority is securing a maximum of freedom. If we could do so, the criterion would still be difficult to apply, since one man's freedom may conflict with another's. Restricting the freedom of factory owners can extend the freedom of workers; for the freedom that the factory owner once had, to hire and fire as he pleased, meant that the worker often did not have the freedom to earn a living. One could say that all extensions of State activity restrict freedom for some in order to increase freedom for others. But then this implies a principle of justice, that *everyone* has an *equal* claim to a maximum of freedom. So I think it is more sensible to acknowledge the complexity of moral objectives to be pursued by the State, and to say that justice and the common good are not identical with freedom, although they are all closely related.

The idea of using a maximum of freedom as the sole criterion of the limits of State action seems most feasible in the realm of criminal law. There has recently been a brisk debate in England about the proper scope of the criminal law. The main protagonists have been Professor H. L. A. Hart[1] and Lord Devlin.[2] Professor Hart has argued, in the spirit of J. S. Mill, that the

[1] See especially *Law, Liberty, and Morality* (London, 1963).
[2] *The Enforcement of Morals* (London, 1965).

main business of the criminal law is to prevent harm to other people. Lord Devlin thinks that the criminal law does and should go farther in preventing also some conduct that is commonly considered immoral even though it may not cause harm to other people. I think that Professor Hart undoubtedly has the best of this debate in his criticism of Lord Devlin's position, but he does not really lay down a firm criterion himself, for he is not prepared to go all the way with Mill. He accepts the propriety of some 'paternalistic' legislation, e.g. on the control of drugs or on harm done to people with their own consent.[1] A criterion in terms of maximum freedom alone does not suffice even for the criminal law.

Apart from this, it is not clear that one could sensibly try to apply the same criteria to all fields of State activity. In the liberal democracies of the western world, the older branches of the criminal and civil law retain a strong tradition of emphasizing the protection of established rights and freedoms of the individual against interference by the executive arm of the State as well as by other individuals, while the newer branches of the law that deal with economic control and the provision of social welfare are more directed towards the ends of the common good and of justice in a reformative sense. As we have seen in Section 2, in all these fields of State action there is room for difference of opinion about the limits of State authority and about the balance to be struck between the ends of freedom, justice, and the common good. This is one respect in which the distinctions of political parties show themselves; and their disputes on such matters cannot be resolved, though they can be clarified, by philosophical analysis.

However, if we agree that freedom is at any rate *one* highly important objective, we can say that the State ought *not* to intervene in social life to the utmost extent in order to serve the objectives of justice and the common good. And if we also agree that freedom is not the *only* objective, then we can say that the functions of the State ought not to be limited simply to the old negative function of holding the ring for freedom.

[1] Cf. Devlin, *The Enforcement of Morals*, essay 7.

VI DEMOCRACY

1 DEMOCRATIC IDEALS

The distinctive features of democratic government, at least as we understand it in the western world, are intended to secure a maximum of liberty for citizens. Government with its rules of law restricts our freedom to do as we please. Democrats recognize the necessity of this, but they believe that, so far as possible, the rules should be self-imposed or at any rate should be in accordance with the will or consent of the citizens. If a man imposes a rule on himself, or agrees to its imposition by another, he is not being compelled but is acting voluntarily. Democracy is a doctrine of 'do it yourself', and, as someone has remarked, 'do it yourself' often comes to 'rue it yourself'. The democrat is prepared to make his own mistakes rather than to be directed by someone else who may have superior wisdom. The underlying idea is that self-direction, choosing for yourself, is far preferable to having decisions made for you, and imposed upon you, by another. This is why liberty is valued.

For the democrat, liberty goes along with equality. He believes that everybody, or at least every adult, is capable of exercising the power of self-direction and should be given the opportunity to do so. The democrat holds that all men have an equal right to liberty and self-direction.

Liberty and equality are what distinguish the democratic ideal from other political ideals. A notion of equality of some sort must figure in any concept of justice, but it figures most prominently in the democratic concept of justice. Liberty and equality are the distinctive aims of democracy. That this has always been so may be seen from the criticisms of democracy made by Plato.[1] Plato describes the ends of democracy as liberty, equality, and variety, and he criticizes democracy precisely because these are its leading features. Liberty, in the sense of doing what you like, is attractive, Plato says, but it cannot last; and it is further-more less desirable than doing the right thing, even though most people, not being wise enough to know and to choose for themselves what is right, have to be directed by others. Equality, in his opinion, is wrong because it goes against nature; men are unequal in their capacities and should be given different func-tions in accordance with their different capacities. (Variety he considers objectionable because it runs counter to an integrated society.)

I have been speaking of democratic aims or ideals, and we often do use the words 'democracy' and 'democratic' to refer to these ideals, or even to one of them alone, especially equality. The latter tendency is particularly common in a country like New Zealand which is strongly imbued with equalitarian senti-ments. When I spent some years in New Zealand after the Second World War, I found people there ready to call the British Civil Service 'undemocratic' because it had a direct entry of university graduates to its policy-making grade, the Administrative Class. Or again, a good many New Zealanders were inclined to say that the British system of university edu-cation was 'undemocratic' because it was more selective than their own in its qualifications for entry. By 'undemocratic' they meant unequalitarian. But they are not alone in this usage. When I first read a well-known *History of Political Theory* by an American scholar, Professor George H. Sabine, I was puzzled by his statement, in the chapter on liberalism, that John Stuart Mill's essay *On Liberty* 'was in a sense a defense of liberty against democracy'.[2] This struck me as virtually self-contradictory until

[1] *Republic*, VIII (557–65).
[2] 1st ed. (New York and London, 1937), p. 667; apparently omitted in the revised edition.

I recalled Alexis de Tocqueville's characterization of *Democracy in America* as the cult of equality more than of liberty. In other circles or in other contexts, however, the adjectives 'democratic' and 'undemocratic' may refer rather to the prevalence or curtailment of liberty. That is why it seems so odd to us that communist régimes should call themselves 'people's democracies'. The communists themselves would no doubt justify their use of the term on the grounds that their form of society is equalitarian and that it serves the interests of the masses instead of (as they think western democracy does) the interests of 'the bourgeoisie'.

There is, then, one usage of the words 'democracy' and 'democratic' which connotes certain social ideals. As contrasted with this usage, however, there is another, in which 'democracy' means a set of political institutions. People who disagree with the so-called 'democratic ideal', and especially with the ideal of equality, sometimes protest sharply against the use of the words 'democracy' and 'democratic' to describe general social aims; democracy, they insist, is a form of government. Etymologically the word 'democracy' undoubtedly began as the name for a form of rule, 'rule by the people', as contrasted with 'aristocracy' or 'oligarchy' (rule by the best men, or by a few), and with 'monarchy' (rule by one man). My reference to Plato, however, shows that, almost from the start, the word 'democracy' was associated with a set of ideals as well as with a form of government. This is intelligible enough, for democratic forms of government will have been adopted only because it was thought that all citizens equally had a claim to self-direction, i.e. because of a belief in a right to liberty and equality. The concept of aristocracy can be similarly used to mean a social ideal as well as a form of government. The 'aristocratic' ideal values culture (by which I mean the pursuit of knowledge and beauty) more than an equalitarian conception of justice. A modern example of the expression of aristocratic values, such as Plato held, is to be found in Clive Bell's book *Civilization*, but there have been plenty of other people who share this outlook, although it is not often boldly acknowledged in opposition to equalitarian ideas of justice.

I have spoken of 'social' rather than of 'political' ideals. The 'democratic' values of liberty and equality are not simply political principles. I mean by this that they do not apply solely to the organization of the State. We may think there should be equality of opportunity in education, without necessarily implying that the whole of the educational system should be run by the State. We may think there should be equality between the sexes, not only in political matters like having the vote or in legal rights to property, but also in regard to opportunity for careers or to equal pay for equal work or to the position of husbands and wives (or sons and daughters) in the family. Similarly, questions about freedom arise in communities and associations other than the State. Just as the laws of the State may restrict freedom (or enlarge it for some by restricting it for others), so the rules, customary practices, and beliefs of churches, educational institutions, industrial and commercial bodies, and of families, may restrict or enlarge freedom for their members. As we saw in Chapter II, Section 3, when discussing patterns of regulation, it cannot be taken for granted that if one thinks a democratic form of organization best for the State, one must necessarily think it best for every kind of association or community. An equal voice for each adult member of a church or a university or a factory is not necessarily the best way of running its affairs. Sometimes a non-political association or community can give its members more freedom, sometimes it must be satisfied with less, than we think it proper and practical for citizens to have in the State. The fact remains, however, that if we accept 'democratic' ideals, liberty and equality are values for us in other spheres of social life too. They may have to be qualified for the sake of other values, just as happens in political affairs; but they remain values to be taken into account.

There is another concept that goes along with liberty and equality in at any rate one strand of democratic thought, the concept of fraternity. The slogan of the French Revolutionaries was 'Liberty, Equality, Fraternity'. The concept of fraternity, the brotherhood of mankind, and *a fortiori* of the members of a particular national community, expresses the idea of common responsibility, responsibility for others, while the concept of liberty expresses the idea of responsibility for oneself. There can be a tension between these two responsibilities, and I think it is fair to say that if we take communism at its best it emphasizes fraternity, while the traditional western notion of liberal democracy emphasizes liberty. This, however, is treating communism as based on ethical principles, an interpretation which would be rejected by orthodox Marxism, which distinguishes itself from what it calls 'utopian socialism'.[1]

Within the western conception of democracy, we may say that democratic socialism emphasizes equality and fraternity, and is apt to lay less stress on liberty than do liberalism and conservatism. Modern democratic socialism also shares with communism a doctrine of economic organization. It accepts the Marxist thesis that the way to reach social improvement is to abolish certain (not all) forms of private property; it advocates public ownership of the means of production, distribution, and exchange. How then does it differ from Marxist communism? The difference is that modern democratic socialism shares the conviction of pre-Marxist socialists or communists that political policy should be rooted in ethical ideals, and especially in a notion of social justice. Like other democrats, socialists found political aims on ethical aims. Marxist communism takes the view that a socialism of this character is useless, unrealistic, 'utopian'. Instead Marxist theory purports to derive its political policies from a 'scientific' sociology; it tries to found politics on science.

2 DEMOCRATIC GOVERNMENT

Abraham Lincoln in his Gettysburg Address described democracy as 'government of the people by the people for the people'. But all government is government *of* the people; and a benevolent despotism, as much as a democracy, may be government *for* (i.e. in the interests of) the people, though the political experience of Europe, if not perhaps always of Asia, leads one to doubt

---

[1] Cf. Friedrich Engels, *Socialism: Utopian and Scientific.*

whether a despotism can for long remain benevolent. The essential idea of democratic government is government *by* the people. Strictly speaking, government by all the people should mean unanimous decisions. But this, of course, is impossible in political matters. Democracy in practice has to mean following the view of the majority. Perhaps Lincoln's addition of 'for the people' means, as in Rousseau's theory of the general will, that the decisive view, which for practical purposes must be that of the majority, should seek to serve the interests of all even though it does not have the agreement of all; otherwise there is the danger, so much feared by de Tocqueville and John Stuart Mill, that majority rule may become majority tyranny.

Pure democracy, a system in which all citizens may join in taking governmental decisions, is rare. It is impracticable except in a very small polity. It was practised, more or less, in the city-state of Athens over a relatively short period. Decisions were taken by the Assembly, membership of which was open to all adult male citizens (but not to women or slaves or resident aliens). Even in Athens many matters of detail had to be left to appointed officers, but these were, for a time, selected by lot, thus preserving the idea that everybody was capable of doing the job and that there was 'no damned merit in it'. Important decisions were taken by the Assembly as a whole.

In most democratic States, however, democracy has meant representative government. The ordinary citizen comes into the process only by casting a vote in favour of a representative or of the broad policy of a party. Decision on concrete issues is left to the body of elected representatives, the Legislature, or to a smaller group, the Government or 'Executive', acting with the consent of the Legislature. So what we have in practice is oligarchy, government by a few, but an oligarchy elected by the people as a whole and responsible to the people as a whole, responsible in the sense that it can be turned out at the next election and replaced by a different group of rulers. Vestiges of pure democratic procedure are found in some States where a popular referendum is held on certain basic issues, but generally speaking democracy in the modern world means representative government, the democratic element consisting in popular election and the possibility of dismissal.

The original idea of a representative was of a person elected to express or reflect (to re-present) the views of his constituents. But this is not practicable either, for it would require the representative to gather together a meeting of his constituents and ascertain the majority view among them before he voted on any issue in the legislative assembly. Every issue would need to be voted on twice, first at the various constituency meetings, where debate on it would take place, and then secondly at the legislative assembly, where the representatives would simply act as rubberstamps recording the majority decisions of their electorates. This is what now happens at the election of an American President, though it was not the original intention of those who drafted the Constitution. A voter in the American Presidential election is really casting his vote in favour of one of the candidates for the Presidency, but formally he votes in favour of a candidate for the Electoral College. The Electoral College then meets to elect the President, but this is simply a process of rubber-stamping, since the Democratic and Republican members of the Electoral College are respectively pledged to vote for the Democratic or Republican candidate for the Presidency, so that the popular election has already determined the issue. Of course this means that there is really no need for the Electoral College; the popular election might as well be formally, as it is in fact, a choice between the candidates for the Presidency. On such a clear-cut issue, coming up for decision once in every four years, there is usually no difficulty in ascertaining the voice of the people. But it would obviously be impossible to refer every concrete issue of policy to the votes of constituencies throughout a country. The idea therefore arose that the representative was chosen, not as a mirror of electoral opinion in his constituency, but as a man of good judgement who could be trusted to make up his own mind conscientiously; he was not to be a postman for the majority of ordinary citizens in his constituency, but a reasonable example of how the ordinary citizen would (or should) decide on a disputed question. The case for this view is put most strongly in a speech of Edmund Burke to the electors of Bristol in 1774. Burke drew a distinction between a 'representative' and a 'delegate'. As he used the words, a delegate merely mirrors and records the views of his constituents, while a representative is elected to judge according to his own conscience. (The members of the Electoral College in the United States were originally intended to be representatives in this sense, but have come to act simply as delegates.)

Now if the members of a legislature really are representatives in Burke's sense of the term, there will be no fixed body of majority opinion. On one issue A will vote with B, and on another issue he will vote against B, just because they are different people with differing experiences and therefore differing views. In these circumstances the Government, the body of policy-makers, will have no guarantee of a majority in the legislative assembly for all, or even most, of its proposals. It will be a weak, unstable Government. On the other hand, a well-disciplined party system makes for a strong, relatively stable Government. The growth of the party system has meant the decline of Burke's idea of the representative. A member of a legislative assembly who is elected on a party ticket is neither a delegate, acting as a rubber-stamp for his constituents, nor a representative in Burke's sense, exercising individual judgement on all issues. To a considerable extent at least, he is simply a yes-man for his party. A nearly always votes with B, Tweedledum with Tweedledee. Occasionally the Members of Parliament in Britain are allowed a 'free vote' on a major issue where the division of opinion cuts across party lines, but the frequency of the occasions seems to be dwindling. The situation of voting according to party is accepted because it makes for more efficient government. But it seems that a large minority, both of elected representatives and of electors (indeed the minority party may have received a majority of the total of votes in the country as a whole, though not a majority of seats), will find their opinion pretty constantly outvoted by the party in power, so that their views seem to count for nothing in the actual decisions of government.

The traditional defence of democratic government tells us

that the opinion of the minority does have some effect. The function of the minority in the legislative assembly, it is said, is to voice their opposition, to criticize, to show the possibility of an alternative policy, so that the dominant opinion should be required to produce a reasoned case for its alleged superiority to the minority view. An essential feature of democratic government, the argument proceeds, is that it is government through discussion, by persuasion instead of by force. When the discussion has gone as far as it usefully can, and some are still unpersuaded, a vote is taken and the majority decision followed, again instead of resorting to force: 'we count heads instead of breaking them'. Voting is, in a sense, a confession of relative failure, the ideal being to reach unanimous agreement, but since that is unattainable the second-best course is to follow the majority view.

This picture of parliamentary debate as a genuine attempt to persuade would be all very well if the participants really were representatives in Burke's sense. It does apply, in the British Parliament, to debates in which there is a free vote and to some of the discussions of details of Bills at the Committee stage. But where there is a strong party system, the broad pattern of voting on any major issue is a foregone conclusion. In the British system of government, the real decisions on major issues are taken by the Cabinet, not by the majority of elected members of the legislative assembly. Still, opinion within the majority party, at least, has its effect on Government policy. The effective criticism is not necessarily that which takes place in public at the open debates of the legislative assembly, though this does count for something despite the fact that the critics within the dominant party usually end up by voting for the Government. In a democratic system of government there is always the possibility of revolt within the dominant party, and (to take Britain again as an example) the Cabinet has to carry with it most of the back-bench M.P.s of its own party in the discussions that take place off the floor of the House of Commons. The leaders of a party can exercise a good deal of control, but it is by no means absolute. In March 1967, Mr. Harold Wilson tried to threaten Labour M.P.s who abstained from supporting the Government in a vote on an important issue of foreign policy. 'Every dog is allowed one bark,' Mr. Wilson told them, 'but if he barks too often he won't get his licence renewed'; a remark which provoked the riposte: 'The Prime Minister does not license us, we license him'. The mere fact that M.P.s can and do sometimes abstain from voting for the party line, even if they rarely vote against it nowadays, shows that a Government can go too far in treating its back-benchers as lobby-fodder.

Yet although a Government has to take account of opinion within its own party, it need not take much notice of the views of other parties in its day-to-day business. Criticism of Government policy by a party in opposition is not made with any expectation of persuading the Government to mend its ways, but rather in the hope of persuading the public to make a different choice at the next election. The Opposition takes the opportunity at every important debate of showing where it stands and what it would try to do if it were in power. Parliamentary elections are not won and lost in the brief period of the electoral campaign, but over the life of a Parliament between one election and another; and while the loss of popular support for a Government is due to its own mistakes or bad luck or the sheer feeling that it is time for a change, rather than to the criticism of Government policy by the Opposition, nevertheless that criticism does help to focus the shift of public opinion and to give it concrete shape. It is still fair to say, therefore, that discussion is an essential part of the democratic process.

The various devices of democratic government—decisions by majority vote; periodical popular elections, with the possibility of throwing out the group now in power; regular meetings of representatives, with continual discussion and criticism, the voicing of grievances and of alternative lines of policy—all these devices are intended to prevent governmental action from restricting liberty more than it need. They give opportunities to those who do not govern to say what *they* would like to be done. It is recognized that government must be carried on by a small group, to whom considerable authority is entrusted. But it is also recognized that the wielder of authority is always liable to suppose that he knows best what is good for the people, or even what the people want; he is apt to suppose that they must want what he thinks will be best for them. The devices of democratic government act as checks on this tendency; they ensure reference back to the people or their representatives at frequent intervals.

A further device, not necessarily 'democratic' in form but similarly serving the democratic aim of checking authority and protecting liberty, is the so-called separation of powers. Government works by law. This entails the making of laws, the application and enforcement of the laws, and at times the interpretation of the law. We may therefore speak of three functions in connection with the exercise of governmental power: the legislative function, the executive function, and the judicial function. (1) Legislative function: some body of persons must be authorized to make new laws and revise or repeal old ones, to declare what the law shall be. (2) Executive function: some body of persons must be authorized to give effect to the laws and to their enforcement. Officials (in the civil service or in local government) must be authorized to tell individual citizens that a particular law applies to them in such and such a way, e.g. to send out income-tax return and assessment forms, to put up 'No Parking' notices, and so forth. Other officials (the police) must be authorized to warn and arrest those who appear to have broken the law. Others again (in the penal services) to carry out the penalties prescribed for law-breaking. (3) Judicial function: some body of persons must be authorized to interpret the law, to decide whether or not someone accused of a crime or a civil wrong has or has not broken the law, and to decide also, in disputes between citizens (or between a citizen and a branch of the Executive), whose claim shall be held to be legally valid. These three functions can of course all be carried out by one and the same body of persons. In a monarchy properly so called, the King has authority to do all these things: and in a 'constitutional monarchy', such as we have in Britain, the *forms* of the older situation are still preserved, as when the last act in the process of legislation is called 'the

Royal Assent'; the Executive acts in the name of 'the Crown'; and the judges are said to represent 'the Queen's justice'. In democratic constitutions, however, there is a certain degree of separation of these functions, which are allotted to different authorities relatively independent of each other.

In the eighteenth century, when the liberty enjoyed in Britain was much admired and envied on the Continent, the French theorist Montesquieu put forward the doctrine of 'the separation of powers', i.e. of the three 'powers' or authorities, legislative, executive, and judicial. Montesquieu's thesis was that such a separation was the best guarantee of liberty for the subject, and he argued that the relatively high degree of liberty in England was due to the fact that the three powers were there kept separate from each other. The English Constitution was a system of checks and balances, in which each of the three powers had its allotted place and could prevent either of the others from going beyond its proper role. Montesquieu concluded that a separation of powers ought to be practised in any State seeking a maximum of liberty. The influence of his theory is to be seen especially in the Constitution of the United States, where there is a clear separation of powers together with a system of checks and balances. In Britain there is not at the present time a separation of all three powers, and there is some dispute whether Montesquieu was right in believing that the Legislature and the Executive in the England of his time were effectively separate authorities. What Montesquieu regarded as most important, however, was that the Judiciary should be independent of the other two powers, and there is no doubt that this both was then and is now true of the British Constitution. To-day at least, whatever the position may have been in the eighteenth century, the men at the top of the Executive, the Government, are not only members of the Legislature but control it. Parliament has only a moderate degree of independence from the Cabinet. But the Judiciary really does act independently from Parliament and Executive alike. The fact that some of the judges are members of the House of Lords is not significant. When they take part in debates, e.g. on law reform, they speak with complete independence; and of

course when they sit in their judicial capacity, the pronounce-
ments of 'the House of Lords' as the highest court of appeal have
nothing at all to do with the proceedings of the House of Lords
as the second chamber of the Legislature. A more significant
fact is that judicial decisions quite often have the effect of revising
and not only of interpreting the law. Law is made by judges as
well as by Parliament. But the law-making activities of Legis-
lature-cum-Executive in the field of statutes and statutory in-
struments on the one hand, and of the Judiciary in the field of
common law on the other, are kept separate from and independent of each other. What is most important of all is the
independence of the Judiciary vis-à-vis the Executive in interpreting the law as it is applied by civil servants to individual
citizens. This has undoubtedly been a bulwark for preserving the
liberty of the subject against the excessive exercise of power by
the Executive.

To some extent Members of Parliament perform a similar
function in certain activities in which they remain representatives in Burke's sense and are not restrained by party allegiance.
I am thinking chiefly of Parliamentary Questions and Debates
on the Adjournment.[1] When these concern general issues of
Government policy, the Minister who replies will usually give
no ground; the situation differs little from a debate on a Bill or
on a motion sponsored by an official Government or Opposition
spokesman. But when they concern grievances of private citizens,
there is some room for probing criticism that may have an
effect on the decisions of senior civil servants, at least for the

---

[1] Readers who are unfamiliar with British parliamentary practice
may wish to know what these two things are. Parliamentary Questions
are questions put to Ministers, with advance notice, by Members of
Parliament and are answered at Question Time, often the liveliest
part of the day's business in the House of Commons. Debates on the
Adjournment take place during the last half-hour of the day's business
in the Commons and may be initiated by any M.P., unlike most of the
other debates, which are arranged officially on behalf of the Government or of the Opposition Front Bench. Each of the two procedures
affords opportunity for *ad hoc* criticism of governmental administration,
but in an Adjournment Debate both the criticism and the reply can
of course be developed at greater length than at Question Time.

future if not for the case under discussion. The Parliamentary Question, followed up by a shrewd supplementary question, can be particularly effective at times, since the Minister may be made to look foolish on the floor of the House, and no senior civil servant, let alone the Minister himself, is content to let that happen without a blush.

But as the Executive, both Cabinet and civil service, grows inevitably more powerful with the increasing scope and complexity of governmental action in a modern society, it becomes more and more difficult for the ordinary Member of Parliament to criticize effectively the details of administration as it applies to individual citizens. He does not have all the necessary information, and he finds it harder to wheedle this out of Ministers or to make them change their tune. That is why Britain has recently taken a leaf out of the book of some other democratic constitutions by instituting the Ombudsman or Parliamentary Commissioner. The Ombudsman in Scandinavian countries performs the same sort of role as the British Member of Parliament in the Parliamentary Question or the Debate on the Adjournment; but the Ombudsman has the advantage of being authorized to call for the relevant departmental files and to interview the civil servants who have been concerned. The powers of the Ombudsman constitute an additional device to protect the liberty of the subject from the excessive or inequitable exercise of authority by the Executive.

I said in Section 1 that liberty and equality are the distinguishing principles of democracy. Most of the procedures or institutions which I have described in the present section, as being specially characteristic of democratic forms of government, are intended to promote the principle of liberty in particular. The principle of equality finds expression in the general idea of government by all the people, which in practice does not mean participation in government proper but participation in the process of electing a Government. The opportunity to take part is given to every adult citizen equally: one man, one vote; and one vote, one value.

3 DEMOCRACY IN INTERNATIONAL SOCIETY

I said in Section 1 that the democratic principles of liberty and equality do not apply solely to the organization of the State, and this is true likewise of the democratic procedures that give expression to the principles. Both the ideas and the procedures of democracy are applied to communities and associations other than the State and to the relations between States. Democratic notions appear especially in the legal aspects of international relations. 'Democratic ideals' in the relations between States owe something to the analogy of democracy within the State itself, and something to analogy from non-political communities, notably the family.

The idea of an international society of States is at times described by the phrase 'the family of nations' (where 'nations' means States). As in the language of religion, which speaks of the 'fatherhood' of God and the 'brotherhood' of man, a metaphor drawn from the most close-knit form of human community is felt to be best fitted to express the notion of a universal society. To a large extent, of course, this metaphor depicts an aspiration or ideal of the friendly relations that ought to exist, not an account of the actual relations that do exist. Apart from the question of ideals, however, the notion of a family does imply something about facts, namely a common outlook and common traditions. Earlier international societies have not been world societies but they could often be called a family of States in this sense. The Greek city-states, for example, despite frequent wars, formed an international society with a common language, common traditions, and some common religious practices such as a respect for the Delphic oracle and participation in the Olympic Games. Although they never formed any stable federation, they distinguished themselves as Greeks from 'barbarians' (which meant, in the first instance, people who spoke a foreign language). In some degree this affected their behaviour. For example, they were prepared to make slaves of conquered barbarians but not, usually, of conquered Greeks. Similarly the world of medieval Christendom was an international society with a common religion and a common legal system (derived from Roman Law). Modern international society has developed from the medieval one, with the tradition of natural law providing a foundation for international law. This means that modern international society follows the traditions and structure of *European* society. Now the countries of Europe can be called a 'family' of nations or States precisely because they share a common tradition, primarily that of international law. Other States which have entered this international system have had to accept the European tradition. Often this has been no hardship, for the former colonies of European countries have legal systems which are themselves founded on the legal systems of the colonizing States. Thus the United State of America and all the countries of the Commonwealth have legal systems based on English Law, while the former French colonies have systems based on French Law, and so on. In some instances, however, States have had to adapt themselves to the European tradition. China and Japan, for example, are not in any sense members of the original European family.

The European tradition explains why the international society of States includes certain democratic procedures, and why these procedures are accepted by non-democratic countries. One example of democratic procedure arises from the doctrine of the sovereign equality of States. In international law all sovereign States are treated as equal, regardless of size or power. Following from this, each member State of the United Nations Organization has one vote in the General Assembly, and the view of a majority of States in any vote taken in the Assembly is held to be the view of the Assembly as a whole. In some ways this is a misleading practice, but it is accepted by all States as being 'democratic' and as built into the structure of international society.

I have said that international law arose from the medieval European tradition of natural law. There is a difference, however, between the medieval international society and the modern one. The world of Roman Christendom in the Middle Ages was not a single State, but neither was it a collection of sovereign States in the modern sense of the term. Up to the time of the Reformation, the secular ruler of a European country did not possess sovereign (i.e. supreme) authority; he was subject to the superior authority of the international Church. When the national State arose as a sovereign autonomous unit, it was recognized that there still was and must be some form of loose association between States, and this was represented by their common acceptance of international law.

In the thought of political philosophers of the seventeenth century, likes Hobbes and Locke, the notion of natural law, or a law of nature, was connected with the notion of a 'state of nature' that preceded civil society and the positive law of civil society. Consequently Emerich de Vattel, an international jurist of the eighteenth century, put forward the idea that States, whose relations with each other are regulated by something like natural law and not by an imposed and enforceable positive law, are in a state of nature. And because the earlier theorists had spoken of individuals in a state of nature as being free (or independent) and equal, Vattel thought the same must be true of States. States are independent, and must be regarded as equal.

The transfer of the concepts of liberty and equality to international law from the ideas of political philosophers about individual persons, indicates that the international society of States is conceived as analogous to a society of individuals. States are considered, in a sense, as persons. This doctrine has advantages, though it also has dangers. The dangers are familiar to students of the history of political theory, but I think that in legal theory they are slight. Some political philosophers who have thought of the State in terms of an organism have reached the conclusion that the State is an end to which its individual members are means; and so they have regarded the State as a real superperson. But when one says that States are considered in international law as (legal) persons, this emphatically does not mean that they are considered to be real persons. States are purely legal entities; one can even say they are fictions. Lawyers know how to get along with convenient fictions, and are not misled by them. A corporation, for example, can be regarded in law as a person, i.e. as a subject of legal rights and obligations (which, as we have seen in Chapter III, Section 5, can themselves be regarded as fictions if compared with physical powers and bonds); but no lawyer is thereby misled into thinking of a corporation as a real super-person, existing alongside the natural persons who act as the officers of the corporation. Similarly the notion of a State as a person in international law simply means that the State is a subject of rights and obligations—the State, as contrasted with the nation, or with the individual who is the Head of the State, though of course certain individuals, such as the Secretary of State (or Minister) responsible for Foreign Affairs, act in the name of the State when exercising the rights or fulfilling the obligations.

The advantages of the concept of States as persons are that this concept helps to ensure stability. Governments come and go, but if the State, and not a particular Government or a particular Head of State, is regarded as the subject of rights and obligations, then successive Governments inherit the position of their predecessors. It is less easy for a new Government to repudiate obligations undertaken by its predecessor; and likewise it is not legitimate for a foreign Government to say 'We made a treaty with your predecessor, not with you, and so you have no rights under it'.

The usefulness of the notion of continuity, however, does not itself require that the analogy between States and persons should be extended to include the ideas of liberty and equality. In matters other than sovereignty (i.e. supreme legal authority) States are neither free nor equal. We saw in Chapter III, Section 3, that even a Great Power does not have complete freedom of political action unless it controls a world empire, and that the freedom of other States is more obviously limited by the policies of powerful neighbours. States are plainly unequal in military or economic strength and consequently in political influence and freedom of action. But then individuals too are unequal in their abilities and consequently in some aspects of freedom of action. The question is whether there is good reason to ascribe to States a right in international law to a certain kind of independence and equality, as there is presumed, in a democratic State, to be good reason to ascribe to individuals a legal right to certain kinds of freedom and equality.

So far as independence is concerned, I think there is good reason so long as we do not have a form of international organization that can properly be called World Government. The settlement of disputes by legal procedures rather than by force requires that there should be supreme legal authorities. Any movement towards strengthening the authority of international law and international courts as being superior to the authority of national law and national courts is obviously to be welcomed. But in the present condition of international society the doctrine of State sovereignty is needed to preserve a measure of respect for law and order, based on some principles of justice, and to make less frequent the resort by powerful States to force and the threat of force.

What of equality? The concept of States as legal persons of course implies equality before the law. That is to say, an international court adjudicating on a dispute between two States must treat them impartially and pay no regard to their unequal status in power or anything else, just as a court adjudicating on a dispute between individuals must be impartial and pay no regard to their unequal status in wealth or anything else. A right to equality before the law is built into the conceptions of natural justice under which the law operates. In addition to this, the concept of sovereignty implies equality of freedom or independence. A sovereign State is legally free or independent in the sense that it is not subject to a superior authority except in so far as limitations are placed on sovereignty by international law. Now if different States had different degrees of this freedom, it would mean either that some States were partially subject to the authority of others and so were not sovereign, or that they were not impartially treated by international law. A State can of course give up its sovereignty by agreeing to become a constituent member of a federal union and transferring to the federal power some parts of its sovereign authority, e.g. in external relations. It then ceases to be a sovereign State in international law. The legal freedom of sovereign States must be an equal freedom.

The sovereign equality of States is a legal concept, which fits well enough into juridical questions that may arise under international law. What is more dubious is its use for purposes in which political power is bound to count for more than legal status. L. F. L. Oppenheim, in his standard textbook on *International Law*,[1] writes of four important consequences of the equality of States in international law. They are: (1) In questions that have to be settled by consent, every State has a right to a vote and only to one vote. (2) 'Legally—although not politically—the vote of the weakest and smallest State has . . . as much weight as the vote of the largest and most powerful.' (3) No State can claim jurisdiction over another. (4) The courts of one State do not normally question the validity of the legal acts of another State. The third and fourth of these principles in fact relate more to the independence of States, i.e. to sovereignty itself, than to their presumed equality. (Oppenheim himself partly recognizes this when he describes the fourth principle as a 'consequence of equality—or independence—of States'.) The first and second, however, are implications of equality and are direct analogues of democratic voting procedures: 'one State, one vote' (like 'one man, one vote'), and 'one vote, one value'. According to Oppenheim, these principles can be qualified by agreement, and in the case of the vital second principle he explicitly distinguishes between the legal and the political weight of votes.

In the political institutions of the United Nations Organization, the doctrine of the equality of States is accepted for membership of, and voting in, the General Assembly, but not for the Security Council. The General Assembly follows the democratic principles of 'one State, one vote', and 'one vote, one value'. The Security Council, however, tries to make proper allowance for the special position of the Great Powers, or at any rate for those States that were leading powers at the time when U.N.O. was set up. The constitution of the Security Council gives expression to the real political facts, namely that leading powers have always had, and are bound to have, more of a say in the conduct of international affairs than smaller powers have. Consequently the rules for voting in the General Assembly are misleading in hiding the

[1] 8th ed. (London, 1955), edited by H. Lauterpacht, Vol. I, § 115.

inevitable facts about decision-making, and are liable to bring international organization into disrepute. Because of the facts of international affairs, a majority vote in the U.N. Assembly does not bind those who are outvoted, as does a majority vote in a national parliament. The resolutions of the U.N. Assembly constitute recommendations only. Nevertheless it would not be true to say that the democratic procedures of the Assembly are simply a sham, concealing the realities of power. Although the vote results only in a recommendation, a heavy vote in the U.N. Assembly against a powerful State (as in 1956 against the Soviet Union's intervention in Hungary, and against the action of Britain and France in the Suez operation) does on occasion have *some* influence on the policy of that State. One should not exaggerate the limited influence that it has. The Soviet invasion of Czechoslovakia in 1968 suggests that memories of 1956 did not greatly affect the decision of the Soviet Government twelve years later. Still, majority opinion can to a small extent act as a check against the reliance on power alone. The position is not altogether different from the effect of opinion in a national assembly. There, under a democratic system, the vote is formally decisive, but with the modern party system a Government can usually rely on receiving a majority vote; the effective decision is taken by the Government itself before the debate in the legislative assembly. A strong body of dissident opinion in the assembly, whether expressed openly in debate or informally at a meeting of back-benchers, will usually not cause the Government to alter the decision already taken; but it will have some influence on future policy. Of course there is a vital difference between the use of democratic procedures at the national and at the international level, in that a build-up of majority opinion against a Government in a democratic State can unseat that Government at the next election, while in international affairs a Great Power remains a top dog despite adverse world opinion. Bearing all these qualifications in mind, world opinion is not without some effect.

Still, the presumed equality of States is not a very satisfactory way of gauging world opinion. A State with 100 million inhabitants has one vote, and a State with 10 million inhabitants has one vote. If ten States, each having a population of 10 million, outvote a single State having a population of 100 million, the vote is 10 to 1 but the populations represented on the two sides are equal.

It is not easy, however, to find a more satisfactory alternative to the principle of 'one State, one vote'. I have spoken as if world opinion would be best gauged in terms of world population. At first sight this seems sensible, because the principle of 'one State, one vote' is formed on the analogy of the democratic principle of 'one man, one vote'. Now if we were to drop the analogy between a man and a State, and instead were to carry the original principle of 'one man, one vote' into international affairs, we should have to give States voting strength in pro-portion to their populations. Suppose we were to allot one vote for every group of 10 million people. Then (taking U.N. estimates of population in 1966) the United Kingdom, with 54 million inhabitants, would have five votes; the United States, with 196 million people, would have 20 votes; the Soviet Union, with 232 million, would have 23 votes; India, with 499 million, would have 50 votes; and China (assuming she were a member of the United Nations Organization), with 772 million people, would have 77 votes. Would we be prepared to stomach this? If not, why not? The reason is not simply because we dislike the policies of China. We should be uneasy also about granting 50 votes to India, even though we preferred the policies of India to those of China. We should be uneasy because we should feel that most of the 772 million Chinese or the 499 million Indians are not in a position to express an opinion on world issues, while on the other hand quite a large number of the 54 million Britons or the 196 million Americans *are* in such a position. World *opinion* cannot be gauged in terms of world *population*.

If we accept this line of argument, we are presupposing the idea, commonly thought to have been abandoned by modern democrats, that a man is entitled to a vote only if he has a reasonable measure of knowledge and education. In other words, our idea of democracy in the international sphere is one of a limited or qualified democracy. Perhaps this is a sound view in the national sphere also. I imagine that British democrats would not be so ready to give a vote to all adult British citizens if Britain had not had a reasonable system of universal education in force for some time. This prompts the reflection that we should not expect a country like China to practise democracy until the Chinese have had a reasonable system of universal education in operation for some time.

At any rate we can see that the transfer of democratic institutions to the international society of States is not a simple matter. The concept of 'one State, one vote', while manifestly unreal and illogical, fills a gap in the meantime, but one cannot expect it to command much respect. So far as *voting* goes, the supposedly democratic procedure of the U.N. Assembly is a bit of a sham. But not so far as *discussion* goes. Democratic procedure means not only decision by majority vote but also decision after discussion. In the U.N. Assembly, as in a national parliament, sensible opinion and criticism can make themselves felt, irrespective of the numbers of votes that they can command. Democracy is a matter of liberty as well as equality, and liberty includes the freedom to express one's opinions and one's criticisms of those who have the whip-hand.

VII JUSTICE

1 A COMPLEX CONCEPT

To call something just is to express approval of it as being right
in a specific way, but to pin down the specific character is not at
all easy. Justice is a complex concept. It is used both of law and
of social morality, and although the ideas of legal and moral
justice share certain common principles they do not stand in
the same relationship to their respective fields of operation, law
and morals. Then again, justice may be regarded on the one
hand as a concept concerned with the order of society as a whole,
and on the other hand as an expression of the rights of individuals
in contrast to the claims of general social order. Finally, justice
is a Janus-like concept, looking both to past and to future, conserving and reforming.

(1) In the law, the term 'justice' is used to cover the whole
field of principles and procedures that ought to be followed.
The system of law as a whole is often called, in legal parlance,
the system of justice. Lawyers will distinguish 'the principles of
natural justice', as a relatively small, though fundamental, part
of the legal system, from the rest of it, but the distinction here is
not between justice and something other than justice; it is a
distinction between a basic part of justice which may be called
'natural' and the remaining superstructure which is also justice
but dependent on custom, precedent, and enactment. In social
morality, however, justice does not cover the whole field of
principles and actions that are considered right. Justice is the

foundation of social morality, and without it the rest would collapse; but it is certainly not the whole of social morality. We contrast justice with generosity or charity, which we regard as going beyond mere justice. What a man is entitled to as a matter of justice we call his rights. Corresponding to these rights of the potential beneficiaries of just actions, there are duties for the potential agents. Generosity or charity implies duties for agents but not rights for the potential beneficiaries.

The law does not concern itself with the moral duties of generosity. The law protects rights and enforces the duties which correspond to rights. This is not to say that the scope of the law takes in the whole domain of moral justice (or moral rights). We saw in Chapter V, Section 2, that a democratic society, at least, tries to restrict the area of legal (i.e. State) authority in order to leave as much room as possible for liberty, and that many forms of moral wrongdoing can be suitably restrained without resort to legal prohibition. In other instances (e.g. in the discouragement of deceit) the 'rough engine' of the law, as Sir James Fitzjames Stephen called it, is not a practicable method of protecting moral rights, and to invoke it would do more harm than good. However, the moral scope of the law is confined within the area of moral justice. A system of law (*ius*) is concerned with the protection of rights (*iura*). It is therefore intelligible that law should use the term 'justice' to describe the whole of its operations.

Of course this does not mean that anything which goes on in a court of law has to be called just. It can be criticized as unjust either from a moral or from a legal point of view. A law can be called unjust for failing to meet moral ideas of justice; and the administration of law (irrespective of whether the particular law applied to a case is itself morally just or unjust) can be criticized as unjust for failing to meet the standards of fairness required by the procedures of the legal system.

(2) The idea of justice, both in legal and in moral thought, is plainly concerned with the general ordering of society. A breach of that order is called a breach of justice, and penalties for the breach are invoked in the name of justice. The criminal law especially is designed to protect the order of society as a whole.

The punishment of crime is not a matter of giving satisfaction to the victim but one of protecting the social fabric. In so far as the victim of a crime is able to vindicate a claim against the criminal in respect of the wrong he has suffered (and generally speaking the legal provisions for this are far from adequate), it takes the form of obtaining reparation or compensation for loss or damage, and is in no way a satisfaction of any natural desire to see the aggressor paid back in his own coin. In a system of criminal law (as contrasted with a system of vendetta), that natural desire of a wronged individual is merged into the general desire of society as a whole to be protected from such harmful conduct, and punishment is imposed by the authority of the organized society and for the sake of the whole society.

The concept of justice is also used, however, to uphold the rights of the individual, if necessary against the claims of general social order. Often there is no opposition between them; the two go together. Most of the transactions of the civil law, for example, protect the smooth working of society, in matters of contract, avoidance of negligence, and so forth, and at the same time the judgements that are given in the case of disputes or breaches are vindications of the rights of individuals. But sometimes, notably in the work of the criminal law and in the framing of governmental policy, there can be a conflict between general social interest and the rights of individuals, and when that happens it is the latter notion which presents itself to us under the banner of justice. Thus, for instance, no person who is innocent of breaking a law may be justly subjected to punishment, although there are circumstances in which this might be conducive to the general interest and the maintenance of public order. For example, if a particular type of crime is prevalent, and if circumstantial evidence would lead many of the real criminals to think that the person accused has been implicated, then his conviction and imprisonment would act as a deterrent for them to the same extent as the conviction and imprisonment of one of themselves; but though useful, this would be unjust. Again, a man who is guilty of a crime may not justly receive punishment in excess of that merited by his degree of guilt.

This is not to say that the claims of social interest must always give way to those of justice, only that the idea of justice stands up for the rights of the individual, even of a guilty individual, against the demands of utility. The principle that an innocent individual should not be subjected to criminal penalties is made absolute in any civilized system of criminal law by defining 'punishment' as the consequence of (usually wilful) breach of a law. Nevertheless, considerations of general social interest may in exceptional circumstances be held to warrant the detention of a person who has not broken any law. In Britain at the beginning of the Second World War, people of German nationality were confined in detention centres. It was called detention, not 'imprisonment', but for those detained there was not a great deal of difference. For that matter the enforced isolation of people suffering from dangerous contagious diseases is not altogether different from the deprivation of liberty that imprisonment involves. Everybody knows that the measures taken in such instances are dictated entirely by the general social interest and that questions of justice or individual rights are simply swept aside. Hence there is no possibility of linking these deprivations of liberty with ideas of punishment. But even within the penal processes of the criminal law, although the logically necessary connection between the ideas of punishment and guilt places an absolute bar on punishing the innocent for reasons of utility, we do sometimes allow utility to override justice where this absolute bar is not present. If a person is guilty of committing a crime of a kind that is becoming widespread, we tolerate the imposition of 'exemplary' punishment that goes beyond his individual deserts, in order to deter other potential offenders. In admitting that it 'goes beyond his individual deserts' we recognize that there is an element of injustice or unfairness in the degree of the penalty, and we imply some measure of compunction in allowing the claim of utility to prevail over that of justice. The same sort of thing can happen in the formation of a governmental policy which involves questions both of utility and of justice. If a scheme of military conscription in time of war exempts from the call-up men in civilian occupations (such as engineering) that are especially important to the war effort, or if a scheme of demobilization at the end of the war gives priority to those whose civilian occupations (such as building) are especially important for post-war reconstruction, we allow that the national interest requires discrimination, but we do so with some reluctance and we admit that it is unfair to the men who are called up to the forces early and are released late. Justice or fairness to the individual is contrasted with utility or general interest, and whichever of the two is held to prevail in a particular situation, the opposition of principle remains.

In the thought of the ancient Greeks (and no doubt the same is true of most primitive societies), the idea of justice almost always had a reference to social order, or, by a natural transference of ideas, to cosmic order. Justice did not connote the same kind of order for a democratically-minded person as it did for one who favoured aristocracy, but for both it had to do with social order. Although ancient Athens was a more radical democracy than modern democracies, and although the Athenian democrat prized liberty and equality, the idea of the *rights* of the individual does not seem to have developed so as to be given explicit expression in language. If one wanted to translate the noun 'rights' into ancient Greek, no single word would be entirely appropriate and one would need either to make do with a word meaning 'privileges' or else to use a periphrasis.

In Plato's *Republic* there is an idiosyncratic notion of 'justice in the soul' which is compared and contrasted with justice in society. This does not really form an exception to the generalization I have made about Greek thought. Plato's idea of 'justice in the soul' is conceived as analogous to justice in society and still relates to a form of order, harmonious order between the different elements of the soul, as justice in society is, according to Plato, harmonious order between different social classes. Plato's view of justice is in fact an aristocratic one, and part of the point of his analogy between society and the individual is to support his preference for aristocracy. There is no such thing as justice *within* an individual. When the concept of justice relates to an individual, it concerns relationships *between* him and other individuals or between him and a group (including the large group that constitutes the organized society of the State). The rights of the individual that are comprised in one aspect of justice are rights vis-à-vis other persons.

Plato's concept of 'justice in the soul', however, is not designed solely to bolster an aristocratic view of justice in society. It also gives expression to the idea of a spirit of conscientiousness in all forms of moral action. From this point of view it approaches Judaeo-Christian ideas about the authority of conscience and the value of the individual soul, though without the equalitarianism that was implicit in those ideas. They were the notions which eventually brought into full consciousness the aspect of justice that is concerned with the rights of the individual. The idea of rights as such made its first appearance, of course, in the language of the law, and the concept of moral or 'natural' rights, under the rubric of moral or 'natural' justice, was an extension of that. The attachment of the idea of moral or natural rights to the notion of the individual person came to full fruition only in the seventeenth century, when Protestantism upheld the authority of the individual's conscience in matters of religion and morals, and in consequence individualism spread into social and political thought also.

(3) A third dichotomy that needs to be noted is that between justice as a conservative and as a reformative principle. I have already referred to this in Chapter II, Section 5(c), and Chapter V, Section 2(d), when speaking of the functions of the State. Conservative justice protects the established order of society with its established distribution of rights, and in the event of breaches it requires restitution of the *status quo* so far as that is possible. Reformative justice calls for revisions of the social order and a redistribution of rights to suit current ideas of fairness. The second of these concepts is, I think, what people usually have in mind when they speak of 'social justice'. The term 'social justice' tends to issue from the mouths of reformers, and to be regarded with suspicion by those who are satisfied with the existing order. It is not in fact a suitable term for expressing the differences of opinion between these two groups, for the adjective 'social'

has misleading implications in suggesting that reformative justice is social while conservative justice is not. As we have seen, justice always has a social reference in that it concerns the order of society as a whole or relationships between individuals or groups of persons; *pace* Plato, justice never means a virtue that affects an individual agent alone, as the virtues of self-respect and prudence can. And if the intention, in speaking of social justice, is to contrast this with legal justice, it is a mistake to suppose that the justice of the law is always conservative. Quite apart from reform of the law introduced by political process, the system of legal justice is itself apt, in civilized countries, to include procedures for self-criticism and reform. The Supreme Court of the United States has had its periods of conservatism and its periods of remarkable reform. In the history of English Law, the courts of Equity modified the rigidity of common law; and while the courts of to-day leave it to Parliament to make major reforms by way of statute, judges are not averse from reinterpreting old laws to suit modern conditions and modern ideas. It is in general true that common law conserves moral ideas of the past, and that statute reforms the law in the light of moral ideas of the present, but this is not a universal rule.

The fact is that none of the three dichotomies which I have made coincides with any of the others. The distinction between legal and moral justice is not the same as that between the justice of the social order and justice for individuals, nor is either of them the same as the distinction between conservative and reformative justice. Legal and moral justice are each concerned both with an equitable order of society and with protecting the rights of individuals against the demands of society, if need be, as well as against other individuals. Each of the two again has its conservative and its reformative aspect: both law and morals regard it as unjust to violate expectations based on long-standing arrangements; yet both recognize that an established order is always liable to ossify conceptions which have become out of date, and that changes in the character of human life, both material and spiritual, require changes of the social structure. It is obvious, finally, that the distinction between conservative and reformative justice is quite different from that between the justice of the social order and justice for individuals. Conservative justice is concerned both with the preservation of established social norms and with the protection of the freedom, person, and property of individuals. Reformative justice is undoubtedly intended to produce a more equitable society, as the common term 'social justice' implies, but it is equally intended to secure for needy or meritorious individuals the rights to which it thinks they are entitled.

2 EQUITY AND IMPARTIALITY

The idea of justice is often, though not always, roughly equivalent to the idea of fairness or equity. Equity is frequently contrasted with equality. 'Fair shares', for example, are not the same as 'equal shares'. How do they differ? 'Fair shares' depend on merit, need, and capacity, which of course are not equally distributed. It is not fair that idlers should receive as much as the industrious, that those with greater need should be given no more than those with less need, that opportunities should go to those who cannot benefit from them rather than to those who can. (I say 'rather than', meaning that the unfair distribution would actually deprive the capable of opportunities that they could use. We speak of fair and unfair distribution only in the allocation of resources that are scarce. If there is more than enough for everyone to take what he wants, no question of justice arises.) Yet the Latin word '*aequitas*' is simply the noun corresponding to the adjective '*aequus*', and it originally meant no more and no less than simple equality. Furthermore everyone agrees that equality in some sense is central to the idea of justice; equality before the law, for instance, is fundamental to legal justice.

Plato and Aristotle tried to explain the connection between equity and equality by distinguishing 'arithmetical' equality from 'geometrical' or 'proportionate' equality. Arithmetical equality gives equal shares to all alike, irrespective of worth. In the language of Plato and Atistotle, it gives equal shares both to equals and to unequals; or, to echo Jeremy Bentham, it says that 'everybody is to count for one, nobody for more than one'. Plato and Aristotle regard this as a mistaken principle, which they would replace by geometrical or proportionate equality, giving equal shares to equal persons and unequal shares to unequal persons. What they mean is that benefits or responsibilities should be proportionate to the worth (the merit or ability) of those who receive them. As Aristotle puts it,[1] if flutes are to be distributed, they should go only to those who have a capacity for flute-playing; and similarly, a share in ruling should be given only to those who are capable of rule. Arithmetical equality represents the democratic concept of distributive justice, proportionate equality the aristocratic concept. The latter is called a form of equality by Plato and Aristotle because it equates benefits and responsibilities with the worth of the recipients, but of course the distribution which it calls for is an unequal distribution. It is (at least part of) what is commonly meant by equity.

Most modern theorists, even when their political sentiments are democratic rather than aristocratic, seem to agree with the view of Aristotle (Plato is less often cited) that equity is entirely a matter of proportionate distribution and that it does not include any principle of strict equality. Equity allows, or rather requires, discrimination by reference to morally relevant differences, and forbids discrimination in the absence of such differences. It is fair to discriminate in favour of the needy, or the meritorious, or the able, and it is unfair to discriminate between people who are equally needy, equally meritorious, or equally able. The rule is to treat like cases alike and unlike cases differently. Within a particular category of people who are all alike in the relevant respect, equity requires equal or impartial treatment. According to those who follow the view of Plato and Aristotle, there is no positive principle of justice which requires that all human beings, as contrasted with all members of a particular relevant category, should be treated equally. The only thing that needs to be said, they argue, is that in the absence of a known relevant difference, we should *presume* that people belong to the same category.

[1] *Politics*, III. 12.

But one may well ask why. If humanity itself is not a relevant category for equal treatment, why should we presume, in the absence of detailed knowledge, that the people affected by our action are equal in respect of need, merit, and capacity, when we know in general that men are apt to be very unequal in these respects?

What would the supporters of Aristotle say about the principle of equality before the law? Here, so it seems at first sight, is a form of strict equality which everyone accepts as required by justice. A judge should be no respecter of persons. He should not favour the rich, or the noble, or the clever, or even the meritorious, because they are rich, noble, clever, or meritorious. Nor should he favour the poor because they are poor, the lowly because they are lowly. Favour for the rich, etc., would be privilege; for the poor, charity or compassion. Neither would be justice. A judge must be impartial. Impartiality is undoubtedly a requirement of justice, and our example suggests that it is a form of equality as contrasted with the discrimination of equity.

In fact, however, the impartiality of a judge fits into the rule of equity. It does not mean that the judge should treat everyone alike, sheep and goats, innocent and guilty. The judge has a duty to discriminate, but only by reference to 'relevant' differences; and for the judge, relevance is in terms of guilt and innocence (or, in cases of civil law, liability and non-liability), not in terms of rich and poor, noble and lowly, clever and stupid, beautiful and ugly, or even of deserving and undeserving as a general moral category (by contrast with the specific *legal* merits of an individual's case as shown by the evidence). The relevant difference for just discrimination has to be relevant to the matter in hand. For the judge in a criminal court, whose business it is to imprison or set free, the relevant difference is guilt or innocence. For the man who is handing out flutes (or, to modernize Aristotle's example, for the committee which is awarding scholarships to an Academy of Music), the relevant difference is capacity or incapacity for flute-playing. The judge follows the principle of equity that like cases be treated alike and unlike cases differently, with the necessary proviso that the only unlikeness to be taken into account is the one relevant to his function. His impartiality requires that he ignore all differences other than proved guilt. Before a verdict has been reached, he must treat equally all persons charged with an offence, because the law presumes that every such person is innocent unless and until he has been proved guilty. During the hearing of cases, therefore, all accused persons are alike, in the eye of the law, in respect of the relevant quality of guilt or innocence, and consequently they are to be treated alike.

It has been suggested[1] that impartiality is a purely formal principle, a principle of logic, rationality, consistency, one that is not specially concerned with ethics but applies to rationality in theoretical as much as in practical matters. The principle requires us to treat like cases alike and unlike cases differently. It is irrational to accord different treatment to persons who are alike in respect of a relevant quality, just as it would be irrational to call one sheet of paper white and another green when they were in fact alike in colour. Ethical questions may come in, it is said, only when we decide what qualities to regard as relevant for a particular purpose. We make a moral judgement when we decide that need, or merit, or ability shall count as the relevant quality for differentiating the like and the unlike; but the rule of impartiality that like cases be treated alike is purely formal.

This view seems to me to be mistaken. There is more to the impartiality of justice than the rationality of logic. We should say that it is dotty, and confusing, to call one sheet of paper white and another green if they are alike in colour, or to kick one of a row of similar chairs and to bow to another; but we should not say it is *unjust*. Injustice is never simply the same as irrationality. We do not talk about justice, or even impartiality, in describing what we do to material things. Nor, I think, in describing what we do towards animals. It may be inconsistent to pick out for slaughter one fine ox and not another; but would we say it is unjust? We

---

[1] Notably by Professor Ch. Perelman. See, for example, his book *The Idea of Justice and the Problem of Argument* (London, 1963): essay 1, 'Concerning Justice'; essay 3, 'The Rule of Justice'; essay 7, 'Opinions and Truth' (especially p. 132).

may feel it is hard on oxen that they, and not horses, are killed for meat, and we may think there is something *unethical* about killing *any* animals for food; but would we say that men are *unjust* to oxen as compared with horses in eating the one and not the other? The concept of justice relates only to our dealings with human beings, and so must presuppose an idea that there is something special about human beings as contrasted with material things or animals. If the Queen of Hearts in *Alice in Wonderland* were to say 'Off with his head!' of every second gardener or every second croquet-player, that would be unjust; but not if she said it of every second rosebush or every second flamingo. In either event she would be acting irrationally. Irrational or inconsistent action towards members of the same category becomes unjust action only if the category of those affected by it is a category of human beings.

Even in our dealings with human beings, not all forms of differential treatment are regarded as unjust or as showing partiality. Suppose I owe £1 to the milkman and £1 to the butcher. Each of them is in the same category of people to whom I owe £1, so that I ought to treat them alike in paying my debts. I have several £1 notes and lots of florins. I should be treating the two men in exactly the same way if I gave a £1 note to each or if I gave ten florins to each, and I should be treating them differently if I gave a note to one and silver to the other. Would we say that the second course of action was unjust or partial as compared with the first? No, because the value received would be the same in either event. A difference of treatment which does not involve a difference of benefit is immaterial. The point is that the equality of treatment for like cases that justice requires, is a material equality, not a formal one; and what makes my differential treatment of the two men materially equal is the amount of benefit as contrasted with the different forms in which the benefit is conveyed.

In the same way as the conferring of benefit is a material consideration for just distribution, so is the opposite process of conferring burdens. Suppose John and James are two of my students, in the same class and of similar ability. If I set each of them an essay on a different subject but of roughly equal difficulty, this is not unjust. It may not even be irrational, though it can well be called inconsistent. There is more to rationality of action than logical consistency. I may have good reasons for my differential, and inconsistent, treatment of John and James. I may have the perfectly good altruistic reason that if they were to write essays on the same subject they could not easily consult the same books at the same time, since duplicate copies are not available. Alternatively I may have the self-interested reason that I do not want to be bored by hearing the same subject discussed twice. We might hesitate to call this, like the altruistic reason, a 'perfectly good' reason, but the fact remains that self-interest can provide reasons for action and can make a pair of inconsistent actions rational. At any rate my differential treatment of John and James is not unjust. If the two essay subjects are equally difficult, and equally distasteful, neither John nor James will think me unjust or partial. They may think me a beast for setting them essays at all, but not an unjust beast. On the other hand, if I were to set John two essays to James's one, or if I were to give an obviously more difficult subject to John than to James, then John could regard me as unjust. A differentiation of burdens is not unjust if they are equally burdensome. The discrimination is unjust only if it involves a material, not a formal, difference, and what counts as material likeness or unlikeness is the weight of the burden.

Justice and injustice, impartiality and partiality, arise only in our treatment of human beings and only in relation to the conferment of benefits or burdens upon them. No question of justice arises over the action of the crackpot who treats his chairs differently, or of the farmer who treats his cattle differently. No question of justice arises over my differential treatment of the milkman and the butcher, so long as they receive equal benefits, or over my differential treatment of John and James, so long as they receive equal burdens. Impartiality, then, is not a purely formal concept. It is not just a rule of treating like cases alike. It is a rule of treating like *persons* alike in the distribution of *benefits or burdens*. Even in its principle of impartiality, justice goes beyond logic to ethics. It presupposes a particular kind of evaluation of human beings as persons, and it has regard to what they themselves value and disvalue as benefits and burdens.

There is a further limitation on the requirement to be impartial. We are so conscious nowadays of the evils of discrimination that we tend to forget that discrimination does not always call for disapproval. M. René Maheu, the Director-General of UNESCO, is reported, by an official publication of his own organization,[1] to have said, at an International Conference on Human Rights held in 1968, that the Universal Declaration of Human Rights 'denounces all discrimination of whatever kind among human beings'. The Universal Declaration does no such thing. Its most general statement about discrimination or distinction is the first sentence of Article 2, which reads: 'Everyone is entitled to all the rights and freedoms set forth in this Declaration, without distinction of any kind, such as race, colour, sex, language, religion, political or other opinion, national or social origin, property, birth or other status'. The article does indeed require the absence of 'distinction of any kind', but only in reference to 'all the rights and freedoms set forth in this Declaration'.

It would be absurd to denounce 'all discrimination of whatever kind among human beings'. The exercise of discrimination is not always wrong. To say of someone that 'he is a discriminating sort of chap' is a mark of praise, and to say that 'he has no sense of discrimination' is a mark of dispraise. It is wrong for a judge to discriminate except in terms of guilt and innocence, but it would be equally wrong for him to fail to discriminate in those terms. It is wrong for a university teacher, marking the examination papers of his pupils, to discriminate except in terms of ability and industry, but it would be equally wrong for him to fail to discriminate in those terms, so long as he is required to assess students by examinations. People who have a duty to be impartial also have a duty to discriminate for relevant reasons. Apart from this, there are many contexts in which a duty of impartiality simply does not arise. There is nothing wrong in being discriminating in the

[1] *Unesco Chronicle*, June 1968, Vol. XIV, No. 6, p. 217.

choice of one's friends; and having chosen them, it is not unjust
to be partial to one's friends. On the contrary, it would be thought
pretty poor if a man treated his friends no differently from the
way in which he treated strangers—*unless* he were dealing with
both by virtue of holding some office or role of authority, in
which event he would have a duty to exercise the role impartially.

The general rule of impartiality or non-discrimination applies
only in virtue of holding an office or role of authority or guardianship. Such roles are of course not confined to official appointments.
A parent is in such a position in relation to his children, and
consequently, even though he may, like Jacob, love one of his
children best, it is unjust or unfair of him to show special favour
to one child over another; but here again, as in other instances,
it is proper to discriminate for relevant reasons, e.g. to pay
university fees for the one who has the capacity to benefit from a
university education.

We are not only apt to forget that the general duty to be
impartial applies solely to the exercise of a role of authority or
guardianship. One can also forget that this duty is built into such
a role. It was, for example, completely superfluous to suggest, as
did the British Home Secretary in 1968, that the Race Relations
Bill should be accompanied by a special clause in the police
disciplinary code requiring police officers not to discriminate
against coloured persons. Police officers are already obliged by
virtue of their office or role to be impartial, except as between
those who appear to be breaking the law and those who do not.
To tell a police officer that it is an offence for him to discriminate
against a coloured man is like telling the same thing to a judge
or to a Home Office official. The excuse given was that many
coloured people think, rightly or wrongly, that police officers do
discriminate against them. But many coloured people think the
same of Home Office officials. If any policeman or civil servant
does in fact discriminate against a coloured man, he is already
violating a duty of his office and can be penalized for doing so. If,
on the other hand, some coloured people mistakenly imagine
discrimination where it does not exist, their misapprehension will
not be cured by repeating in a special clause a duty that is already

built into the general provisions of the police disciplinary code. This does not mean that there is no point in legislating against discrimination. Not all roles have duties of impartiality built into them. It would be outrageous to legislate against discrimination in the choice of one's friends, but there can be good reasons, in some circumstances, to legislate against discrimination in the choice of one's customers. A shopkeeper does not exercise a role of authority or guardianship; and if he chooses to give credit to his friends and not to other customers, that is his affair. He does not violate any duty of his role (as he would if he were to give short weight). So too, if an employer, or a hotelier, or a property owner discriminates in favour of one group or against another in offering jobs, accepting clients, or selling houses, he is not violating any duty of his role as a businessman. Nevertheless, if for special reasons serious social harm is caused by leaving complete freedom to employers, hoteliers, property owners, etc., in their choice of applicants for jobs or clients for rooms and houses, the State may well be justified in laying upon them by statute a duty of non-discrimination, which they do not have by virtue of their function, as police officers, judges, and civil servants do.

What sort of social harm justifies such legislation? There will not be universal agreement about the answer to this question. As we saw in Chapter V, Section 2, there is liable to be difference of opinion on the extent to which the State should restrict freedom for the sake of worthy social aims. I suggest that legislation against discrimination is justified where the discrimination in question has the effect of depriving a group of people of benefits that are generally acknowledged to be common rights. That is why the Universal Declaration of Human Rights limits its denunciation of discrimination to the field of human or common rights, rights that are considered essential for tolerable human life in civilized society. For example, if there is a widespread practice of discriminating against coloured people in accepting applicants for employment, or in letting rooms in hotels, or in selling houses, this causes grave hardship for a coloured man in finding a job, a bed for the night, or a place to live in. On the other hand, if the discrimination results in annoyance and resentment, but no real difficulty in meeting essential needs, there is insufficient warrant to legislate. For example, if a private golf club discriminates against coloured people (or other minority groups, such as Jews) in accepting applications for membership, this, though morally offensive, does not deprive anyone of common rights or essential needs. The excluded applicants can play their golf on a public golf course; or, if they can afford to join a private golf club, they can presumably afford to set up one of their own; or, at the worst, if no alternative methods of playing golf are open to them, they can take up a different form of exercise or sport. But the coloured man who is excluded from a job, or from a hotel room when travelling, does not have a tolerable alternative. The man who is prevented from playing golf can play tennis instead, or go for a walk, without suffering any serious deprivation; but unemployment or a bench in the park is no substitute for a job or a bed.

Some people will say this does not go far enough. It is all very well to value freedom and to be chary of extending legal restrictions on it, they will argue; but the freedom to exercise prejudice is worse than worthless. Even if a form of discrimination, as in entry to a golf club, does not deprive a man of essential needs, it does harm to the social fabric and should be restrained on that account in the name of justice. But then, where is the line to be drawn, if not at the protection of human or common rights? A group of white Protestant businessmen who set up a golf club may want to keep themselves to themselves and their like in their recreational activities; and so they exclude from membership coloured people, Jews, Roman Catholics, parsons, and lawyers. If such discrimination is to be made illegal, what are we to say of a club set up by Jewish or Catholic teen-agers, which restricts its membership to young people of the same religion? Is it to be compelled by law to admit Protestants, greybeards, or tiny tots? For that matter, is an individual to be required by law not to confine his friendship to those whom he finds like-minded or congenial? Of course this is absurd. Making friends is a two-way process, and generally speaking, a man whom I do not want as a friend will himself not want me as a friend. Yes, and if a golf club practises discrimination against Jews or Roman Catholics, any self-respecting Jew or Roman Catholic will not want to be seen dead in the place. Equally, if a hotel discriminates against coloured men, any self-respecting coloured man will not want to be seen dead in the place—provided that he has a reasonable alternative. The trouble arises when there is no reasonable alternative, when many hotels discriminate, so that the coloured man has no assurance that he can find a room.

Still, the argument about harming the social fabric deserves some further consideration. Suppose there were adequate but separate hotels for coloured people only. Suppose there were adequate but separate schools, swimming baths, factories, for coloured people only. Is it a satisfactory state of affairs to have a social apartheid, with 'equal but separate' facilities for white men and black? A caste system may avoid social tension but it is morally offensive none the less. Since justice concerns the social order as well as the rights of the individual, should we not agree that 'equal but separate' facilities are unjust even when the facilities for individuals really are equal?

The weakness of this objection is its unreality. When it is claimed, in southern states of the U.S.A. or in South Africa, that black men are, or will be, given equal but separate facilities, the truth is that the facilities neither are nor can be really equal. That they are not is obvious to anyone who looks. That they cannot be is due to the fact that there is no equality of choice. The separation is imposed by a more powerful group on a less powerful. However sincerely the white men may aim at equality of facilities, the mere fact that they are the top dogs politically, and have made the decision that facilities should be separate, means that there cannot be true equality. A caste system is morally offensive, not just because it separates different groups, but because it is a hierarchy in which some groups are counted as superior to others. If black men had equal facilities of *choice* with white men, and if both groups voluntarily decided that they would prefer to have separate schools, hotels, etc., would the result be morally offensive? It might be morally unsatisfactory in weakening the sense of fraternity, but it would not be *unjust*.

We might well feel that such a society had become 'two nations', and that a unified society was preferable. The fact is that if my hypothetical example were to be realized, there *would* be 'two nations', which would probably want to dispose themselves geographically and politically so as to form two States, but perhaps combining in a federation for some purposes, such as defence and trade, for the sake of mutual advantage.

A more realistic example of equal but separate facilities is to be found in the educational arrangements which religious minorities can make for themselves, if they choose, in Britain. In a city such as Glasgow where there is a large Roman Catholic minority, the Catholics have the facility of setting up their own schools maintained or supported by the State. Not all Catholics choose to send their children to those schools, but a great many do, and no-one would deny that the education received is as good as that of similar non-Catholic schools. Some people may deplore the separation as being inimical to civic fraternity, and may advocate that religion should be kept out of the schools altogether. On the other side, religious people, whether Catholic or Protestant, will argue that religious education and religious practice are an essential part of education as they see it; and they might well add that this is the best way to foster a spirit of fraternity. However that may be, would anyone say that the separate but equal facilities are unjust or unfair? Unfair to whom? The social dimension of justice is a matter of protecting the fabric of social norms that are accepted by most members of the society as generally advantageous to them all. Where there is mutual agreement to a diversity of arrangements for different groups in order to meet their several interests, there is a departure from uniformity but not from justice.

5 THE RIGHT TO EQUALITY

I have said that persons exercising a role of authority or guardianship have a duty of impartiality built into that role. For persons acting in other capacities there is no such built-in duty of impartiality or equal treatment; but for special reasons such a duty may be laid upon them by statute, as by the Race Relations Act, 1968, to prevent racial discrimination in things like employment, housing, and admission to hotels, or as there might be in an Act requiring equal pay for equal work as between the sexes. Whenever there is a duty of impartiality, whether it is built into a role or is imposed by statute, those affected by the actions of persons having the duty are held to have a right to equal treatment. If I favour my friends in the giving of Christmas presents, I do not breach anyone's rights, for we should not say that anyone had a right to receive Christmas presents. But if discrimination has the effect of depriving some people of facilities that are normally available to anyone, we should be inclined to say that their right to equal facilities with others should be recognized and protected by law.

What are the grounds of the belief that all human beings have a right to equal facilities of some sort, and to what sort of equal facilities do they have a right? It is said, e.g. in the American Declaration of Independence, that 'all men are born equal'. Are they? Men are unequal in capacities, whether of physical strength or of brain, as they are in beauty. It may be 'unfair' of nature to endow them so differently, but the fact is that they are not born with equal endowments. Of course, nobody supposes that they are. The statement 'All men are equal' (or 'All men are born equal') is meant primarily, not as a statement of fact, but as a statement of right: all men have a right to equal treatment (in some sense).

What is the justification for this statement? If men are not in fact equal in their endowments, needs, or merits, why ought they to be treated equally? Some philosophers argue that there is no right to positive equality of treatment, and no factual equality among men on which to base such a right.[1] The claim for so-called equality, they say, is a negative claim for the removal of arbitrary or unjustified inequality. For example, the French Revolutionaries, in demanding equality, were demanding a removal of arbitrary privilege, such as that which confined

[1] See, for example, S. I. Benn and R. S. Peters, *Social Principles and the Democratic State* (London, 1959), pp. 108–11.

political rights to the rich and the well-born. But how can one judge that discrimination is arbitrary or unjustified, based on irrelevant grounds, unless one presupposes a basic equality? To give flutes to those with a capacity for flute-playing is discrimination on relevant grounds. So is giving the vote to those who are capable of exercising it. To give the vote only to the wealthy is arbitrary, because the possession of wealth has nothing to do with the capacity to vote. Now if the French Revolutionaries had urged that votes should be given only to the intelligent and educated, it could be said that they would have been asking for discrimination on irrelevant grounds to be replaced by discrimination on relevant grounds. But if one asserts that voting should not be a privilege of any limited group (except in terms of age), that it should be available to every adult, this surely presupposes the view that all adults have the *capacity* to exercise the vote. So that one *is* implying a belief in a form of factual equality. One is implying that every adult has the capacity to form a political judgement. The belief may not in fact be true. The democrat who advocates votes for all adults may be mistaken in his presupposition, as one would be if one advocated the distribution of flutes (or music scholarships) to everyone. And I have already suggested in Chapter VI, Section 3, that the democrat's view perhaps carries the proviso that capacity to form a political judgement requires some measure of education to be added to universally innate ability. It is clear enough, however, that he presupposes, rightly or wrongly, that the innate ability is universal. Likewise if one says that all persons, irrespective of colour, should be treated equally in regard to opportunities for employment or housing, one is implying, not only that colour is irrelevant to the ability to perform a job or to pay rent for a house, but also that everyone *needs* a livelihood and a home.

To be sure, people are unequal in their capacities and needs; but certain basic capacities and needs are possessed equally by all. When it is said that all men are equal, this means not only that they have an equal right of some sort but also that, despite the many natural inequalities between human beings, they are all equally endowed with certain basic capacities and needs, and that, in some of these shared qualities, they differ radically from other animals. What is this difference? Human beings share with all animals the need for sustenance, and with many animals the capacity to enjoy pleasure and to suffer pain. We also regard some animals as capable of thinking to a certain extent. What we suppose animals do not have is the capacity for *rational choice*. This, *added* to the capacity to enjoy pleasure and to suffer pain, is what we suppose distinctive in human beings. And because every man also has the capacity for imaginative sympathy, for putting himself in other people's shoes, he can understand that other people, like himself, want to live their lives in their own way. Some people are cleverer or stronger than others, so that they can make better use of their capacity for choice. But all can choose, and all can enjoy and suffer. This is what makes our common humanity, and this is the factual basis for the claim that all men have an equal right of some sort.

I turn now to the question, to what do all men have an equal right. Certainly not to equal treatment in all respects and in all circumstances. I shall consider three suggestions, (1) that the right to equality is a right to equal *consideration*; (2) that it is a right to equal *opportunity*; and (3) that it is a right to the equal satisfaction of basic *needs*.

(1) The first suggestion, that the right to equality is a right to equal consideration, seems to me plainly unsatisfactory, for it is too vague to give any substance to the answer we are seeking. To say that someone ought to receive consideration is to say that he ought not to be just ignored. Suppose that I happened to dislike red hair and that, in exercising an office which requires impartiality, I were to discriminate against someone because he had red hair. I could say: 'I *considered* you all right; I considered you just as carefully as the rest. I made a special point of inquiring whether your red hair was natural or dyed, and since I found that it was natural, I turned you down.' It will be said that the possession of red hair is not relevant to the choice I had to make. But in one sense it *is* relevant. A man's likes and dislikes are relevant to the choices that he makes. The point is that when I am choosing in the exercise of an office of authority, I

ought to put aside my private likes and dislikes because my duty is to choose as a public and not as a private person. So it is not enough to say simply that I ought to give equal consideration to the people affected by my choice. This might mean simply that I should spend an equal amount of time or effort in considering them. What is important is that I should consider only those qualities that are relevant to the purpose of the public duty laid upon me. To say that all those who will be affected by my decision have an equal right to consideration, is simply a way of saying that I have a duty to be impartial, to discriminate only in terms of qualities relevant to the role I exercise.

(2) A right to equal opportunity is more substantial and seems more promising as an answer to our question. The suggestion is that everyone has a right to equal opportunities for self-development, to make the most of the capacities with which he is endowed. The idea of equal opportunity can be illustrated especially in education. If all equally are given the opportunity for self-development by way of education, some (those who are better endowed by nature) will be better able to take advantage of it, while others will not; and some (the ambitious and the industrious) will choose to take advantage of the opportunity offered, while others will not. The opportunity will be equally distributed but the resulting benefits will be unequal owing to diversity of talent and of effort (to say nothing of luck).

Equal opportunities need not be identical opportunities, and diverse talents need not be unequal talents. If two different things are to be called unequal, the difference must be a quantitative difference in a qualitative likeness, so that they can be placed on the same scale. It makes sense to say that ten years of education are unequal to twenty, or that an Intelligence Quotient of 100 is unequal to an I.Q. of 150. We are rating two things of the same sort on the same scale. But it does not make sense to say that technical education is unequal to musical education, or that a talent for carpentry is unequal to a talent for playing the violin. They are different kinds of education or talent, and since they cannot be put on the same scale they cannot in themselves be called unequal. But if the one talent and the one form of education lead to an occupation bringing in a wage of £20 per week, while the other lead to an occupation bringing in a wage of £40 per week, the monetary receipts are unequal, and that inequality tends to produce a rating of the two occupations, and of the two types of talent and education, in terms of the monetary receipts. The inequality is due to social arrangements, not to the sheer difference between the occupations, talents, and forms of education. And the inequality of pay and status in the social arrangements is due to economic considerations of utility and scarcity. High pay and high status are given to doctors because the work of the doctor is highly useful and because relatively few people are capable of doing it. Consequently a distribution of opportunities that are equally suited to different (but not unequal) natural talents may result in unequal (not just different) rewards.

When people speak of equal opportunity, they often have in mind, not the differentiating of opportunity to suit different capacities, but rather the equalizing of opportunity to compete for relatively scarce positions of high pay and status. In particular, they have in mind the removal of those restrictions on opportunity that are due, not to differences of natural capacity and the social arrangements that follow from the utility and scarcity of certain capacities, but to other social factors. Two boys may have roughly the same degree of the same sort of ability which could lead to well-paid jobs. But they may receive different, and unequal, educational opportunities because the father of one boy is rich, knowledgeable, and keen on giving his son a good education, while the father of the other boy is poor, ignorant, and uninterested in education. Hence the advocacy of 'equal opportunity', meaning that educational opportunities should be related to ability and not to social background.

But is not this idea of equal opportunity liable to be self-defeating? Suppose it could be arranged that all the children of one generation in a particular society should start equal in the race. Those who have greater ability (in terms of socially useful and relatively scarce talents), and who put forth greater efforts, will become better off and more knowledgeable. What about their children? The successful man, wealthy and knowledgeable, will wish to give better opportunities to his children, and he will be in a better position to do so than the unsuccessful man. Even if private, fee-paying schools have been abolished, the wealthy man will be able to give his child more books, more travel, more culture generally. Is the Government to strip him of his wealth in order that his child shall not have these advantages? If so, and if he knows beforehand that the fruits of his success will be taken from him, he will have little incentive to make the most of his abilities. In any case, even if he is stripped of his wealth, he cannot be stripped of his knowledge, which in itself gives his child an advantage.

Another feature of this idea of equal opportunity is that it implies a notion of competition. I said just now: suppose all the children of one generation were to start equal 'in the race'. The idea of equal opportunity seems to be tied to that of a race to get to the top, a race for the 'glittering prizes' of wealth and prestige. It is one thing to speak of fitting opportunities to talents so that everyone can realize his capacities for a full and enjoyable life. It is another thing to speak of equal opportunities to compete for the prizes of society as we know it, and notably for wealth. Is this really the sort of thing that equalitarians are after, when they advocate 'social' or reformative justice? Do they object to the prominence that is given to the social prizes of wealth and prestige, or only to the way in which these are at present distributed? Do they, like Plato, want the 'naturally superior' people to be socially superior?

Then again, if it is thought unfair that social arrangements should favour some rather than others, why stop at social arrangements? Is it not unfair that nature gives more brains or more beauty to some than to others? Why should it be considered particularly just or fair to accommodate social arrangements to those of nature? We do not always think it right to follow nature. If disease can be cured or prevented, we think it ought to be, though that means going against nature. If a child is born blind, we are not content to let him bear the whole brunt of the disability with which nature has endowed him, but we try, so far as we can, to mitigate his natural 'inferiority' by making special provision for him.

(3) The idea of equal opportunities is therefore not quite such plain sailing as appears at first sight. Is it in any case enough to satisfy the idea of a right to equality? If owing to ill fortune an individual is unable to take advantage of his opportunities, is it right to let him starve to death? Is it even just? In the days of old-style *laissez-faire* liberalism it was thought that the business of the State was to hold the ring clear for competition, giving everyone equal liberty (a minimal form of opportunity) to do the best he could for himself, and leaving the weak to go to the wall. Charity might rescue the weak, but that was not a matter of justice or rights. The modern Welfare State, however, gives expression to a significant change of outlook. Everyone is thought to have a right to subsistence, even if he has not earned it. In fact the arrangements of the Welfare State imply a right to subsistence not only for the man who has been unfortunate but also for the idler who has chosen not to take advantage of his opportunities. We should not say that the latter *deserves* help, as the former does, but it is still thought that the satisfaction of basic needs is *due* to everyone as a matter of right or justice, and as a duty of the organized community to all its members.

The communist idea of distributive justice is that the distribution of burdens should depend on abilities, while the distribution of benefits should depend on needs: 'from each according to his ability, to each according to his needs'. Merit does not come into the picture. Benefits are not to be the reward of contribution to the common good. It is presupposed that reward is unnecessary, that ideally men can shed their selfishness and contribute to the general interest without thought of a return. In a communist society, it is imagined, men will work for the common good as hard as they can, in the way that their different abilities allow, and that they will be content to receive what they need, not what they have earned. Of course, their needs differ to some extent, and therefore they will not receive identical benefits. A scholar needs books, a scientist needs equipment, and each needs a good deal of leisure and peace. These are needs both for

fulfilling their communal function and for the personal satisfaction that comes from realizing one's potentialities. But in
many respects all men need the same sort of things and have the
same sort of capacities for enjoyment. Thus in a communistic
settlement like an Israeli kibbutz, there are no wages. Everyone
is given the use of a house, access to communal meals, the same
ration of clothing, and the same amount of pocket-money
to spend as he will on books, holidays, or whatever else he
chooses.

The communist notion of distributive justice is idealistic and
can be practised only by relatively unselfish people such as the
members of a kibbutz or of a monastery. It is not practised in
communist *States*, where lip-service is paid to the idea of equality
while incomes can be highly unequal. In George Orwell's
Animal Farm, 'all animals are equal but some are more equal
than others'. The communist slogan may be contrasted with what
Marx regarded as the principle of distributive justice in a socialist
society: 'from each according to his ability, to each according to
his work'. Here benefits are distributed in accordance with a form
of merit. Those who work hard receive more, those who take it
easy receive less. This idea makes concessions to the natural
selfishness of most men as we know them. The incentive of
reward is required to make them give of their best for the common
good. If they are rewarded according to desert, instead of receiving benefits according to need, this will be useful to the
society as a whole since it will be an incentive to them and to
others to put forward their best efforts. The 'socialist' concept of
justice differs from that of *laissez-faire* liberalism in that it
expects men to contribute intentionally to the common good and
to obtain their reward in terms of that contribution and not in
terms of effort made for their own private good.

The Welfare State is an amalgam of ideas drawn both from
liberalism and from communism. (Historically it is the heritage
of radical liberalism.) It assures a basic minimum, the satisfaction of basic needs of subsistence, to all equally, irrespective
of merit or work. But above the line of the basic minimum it
leaves individuals free to compete for higher rewards. Just where

the line of the basic minimum should be drawn is, of course, not clear. Different countries, and different political groups within a country, will take different views of what constitutes the basic necessities of human existence that ought to be provided for all and that can be afforded. For the purpose of our conceptual discussion, however, the point is that the basic minimum is regarded as a right, something required by justice, while above the line of the basic minimum there remains scope for the older liberal idea of leaving a man free to rise or fall by his own effort or lack of it, and by the good or ill fortune of his natural endowments and the chances of personal history and environment.

The equal satisfaction of basic needs does not always imply an equal distribution of the material means to such satisfaction. Everyone needs food to live, but the diabetic needs insulin as well. Every child needs education, but the blind child cannot be educated by means of the normal provision made for other children and has to be given special, more costly, facilities. The needs of the diabetic and of the blind child are greater than those of the normal person, and so the provision for their needs is greater than normal. The distribution of benefits is therefore in one sense unequal. It is an equitable, not an arithmetically equal, distribution, and is intended to be proportionate to unequal needs. Nevertheless this differential distribution is not in accordance with nature, like the differential distribution of opportunities and rewards proportionate to talents and efforts. It goes against nature and implies the view that natural handicaps should be mitigated so far as possible. There is clearly presupposed an idea that everyone has a right to the equal satisfaction, at least up to the point of a basic minimum, of the desire to go on living and to exercise specifically human capacities, even though nature does to give everyone the endowments to do so by normal methods. So there is a sense in which the distribution of *benefits*, of satisfaction received, is equal, although the distribution of *means* to benefit is unequal because of special needs. The right to equality proper, as distinguished from equity as a whole, is a right to the equal satisfaction of basic human needs, including the need to develop and use capacities which are specifically human.

It may be asked how far should this go? When does a general desire become a basic human need? The blind man would like to have the advantages of sight. The ugly sisters would like to have the beauty of Cinderella. Since everyone wishes to be beautiful, is plastic surgery for the ugly to be called a basic need? The answer to this is: sufficient unto the day is the decision thereof. Provision for basic needs as a matter of right is made, in the main, by politically organized societies for their members, and what a particular society counts as the level of basic needs, to be publicly met, depends on its evaluation of competing claims and what it can economically afford. In Britain at the present time, people with poor vision can obtain spectacles as of right under the National Health Service, but if they think that a standard frame will impair their appearance and they ask for a more stylish frame, which is more expensive, or for contact lenses, which are more costly still, they are expected to pay for these aids to beauty. The public authority judges, on behalf of the organized society, that aids to good vision are a basic need while aids to good appearance are not. There are more pressing uses for the taxpayers' money. In many other countries, some richer, some poorer than Britain, the supply of spectacles of any kind is not made a public charge. If and when a particular society can afford to provide plastic surgery for all people with ugly noses, and if the majority of people in that society should come to think that the unhappiness of having an ugly nose makes a decent standard of life impossible, then, in that society, plastic surgery for the ugly will be counted a basic need. But we cannot lay down *a priori* a level of satisfactions which shall be counted as basic needs for all men everywhere. Some, such as protection from bodily harm, are acknowledged by the laws of all civilized States as both necessary and practicable. We can add that if the right to life is everywhere acknowledged as a human right, its fulfilment requires not only that murder be prohibited but also that starvation be prevented. This is not always practicable, however, and a need cannot become a right (of recipience, implying a duty on the part of others) if the satisfaction of it is not possible. In practice, therefore, the standard of basic needs to be met by public action has to be set by each politically organized society for itself, in the light of its own economic situation and its evaluation of competing claims.

Philosophical analysis cannot provide us with a standard of basic needs that is universally applicable. What I have tried to do is to show that the idea of just distribution according to need implies a positive notion of equality of right and a positive notion of factual equality among men. It is not true that the claim of justice for equal treatment (in the absence of relevant reasons for discrimination) is a purely formal claim of rationality or consistency, nor that it is a purely negative claim for the removal of arbitrary inequalities. It does include both of these, but in addition it is substantive and positive, relating to a combination of qualities possessed by all human beings and to a measure of equal satisfactions that are considered due to them in the light of their possession of common human qualities.

4 EQUITY AND UTILITY

An equitable distribution may depart from equal distribution on grounds of need, merit, or ability. We have seen in Section 3 that discrimination on grounds of special need is in fact an attempt to lessen inequalities and presupposes a right to equal satisfactions up to a basic level. The actual distribution is unequal, but the aim of it is to reduce inequality. This is not true of unequal distribution on grounds of merit or ability.

With all three grounds for discriminatory treatment, one may ask how far the justifying reason for discrimination is one of utility. As I mentioned in Chapter IV, Section 6, Utilitarians hold that all principles of justice derive their moral force from being means to the general interest. The utilitarian view may be most easily illustrated in the case of distribution according to merit. Actions and dispositions that are called meritorious, or deserving of reward, are usually beneficial to society, and those that are said to deserve punishment are usually harmful to society. If a particular meritorious act does not in fact benefit anyone, as when a heroic attempt to save a drowning man is unsuccessful and perhaps results in the death of the would-be rescuer too, it may still conform to a version of the utilitarian theory because it is an example of a type of action that usually has beneficial results. The Utilitarian further holds that reward and punishment are themselves warranted by their utility. The one encourages, the other discourages, repetition of the kinds of actions that are rewarded and punished.

Much the same would be said by the Utilitarian about discrimination in favour of people with unusual ability, who are in fact often said to 'merit' or 'deserve' their special benefits or opportunities. Generally speaking, it is useful scarce abilities that receive special treatment. A person with a bent for mathematics will be offered a university education to develop his talent and a well-paid job in which to exercise it. A person with a bent for strangling or for blowing safes will find no such encouragement.

Even discrimination on grounds of need depends on utility, according to the Utilitarian. People who are not at work, either because no suitable job is available or because they are temporarily sick or permanently disabled, are not at present contributing to the general welfare of society. There is a good chance of their making such a contribution in the future, if they are given enough money to keep alive, and if meanwhile the unemployed are trained for a new kind of job, the sick are given medical attention, and the disabled are provided with special equipment. If their needs are not met, there is no chance of their being useful to society. They will either be a continuing burden or will simply die off and be neither useful nor burdensome.

Such is the utilitarian thesis. It is strongest on merit and weakest on need. To see its weakness on need, consider the example of people who are too old to work, or of people who are permanently disabled in such a way that they cannot be equipped to do a socially useful job. Would we think that they have no right to provision for basic needs?

Some people would say that the elderly have a right to an

old-age pension only if they have earned it by the work they have done in the past (or else a straightforward contractual right in return for monetary contributions), and that the disabled likewise have a right to a pension only if they have merited it, e.g. if the disablement is due to war service; but that the elderly and the disabled who have not earned the right by publicly useful work or service have no right at all. According to this view, the rights of need are rights of merit, and where there is no merit there is no right; to provide for needs in the absence of merit is an act of charity, not of justice.

If this position is taken up on behalf of Utilitarianism, we must of course add that the rights of the old-age pensioner and of the disabled ex-serviceman are to be understood in utilitarian terms: the service which they performed was socially useful, and it is socially useful to reward them *pour encourager les autres.* Does the Utilitarian then think that the ex-serviceman who is not in need has as much right as the ex-serviceman who is? The ex-serviceman who is disabled or too old to work has a greater claim on the community than the disabled or elderly man who is not also an ex-serviceman; for the former has a claim of merit as well as a claim of need. But it is also plain that the ex-serviceman who is disabled or otherwise in need has a greater claim than the ex-serviceman who is not; the former has a claim of merit and need, the latter one of merit alone. It would be very odd to say that the *merit* of a soldier is redoubled by the ill fortune of disablement during service. His claim on society is redoubled, and it is now a claim of two different kinds, merit and need.

We must therefore reject the suggestion that the claims of need, when they are claims of justice and not appeals to charity, are claims of merit. This being so, there is less reason to accept the further thesis that need without merit, though a proper subject for charity, gives rise to no claim of justice. For if we say that the congenitally disabled man has no claim of justice simply in virtue of his need, we must also say that the disabled ex-serviceman has no greater claim than the ex-serviceman who is not disabled. I have assumed all along that the judgements we commonly make in terms of equity or fairness do make special provision for need as well as for merit, i.e. that need can give rise to a claim of justice. The theory of Utilitarianism itself does not deny this, but tries to interpret the claim of need in the same sort of way as the claim of merit. That, we have seen, will not do.

What the utilitarian account omits is the thought that a human being has a claim on fellow human beings simply by reason of human nature and fellowship. When we judge that equity requires special provision for special need, we are thinking of what is owed to someone as a person, as an 'end-in-himself' (to use the language of Immanuel Kant). This means that the fellow members of his society, whether it be a family, a religious community, or a Welfare State, think that they have a strict duty to him as one like themselves and one of themselves, a being with ends or purposes which they, in a measure, adopt as part of their own ends. Justice, unlike some other moral virtues, does not require social responsibility for need to go beyond a certain minimum. What it does require, it requires as due to the individual person and not as a means to the future benefit of the whole society.

Regard for the claim of ability likewise includes the thought of what is due to the individual person as an 'end-in-himself'. Undoubtedly there is also thought of social utility. That is why special provision is readily made for talents that are useful to society while no provision at all is made for those that are harmful to society. But social utility cannot account for the whole of our regard. In a school, for example, provision will be made, if it can be afforded, for developing (a) talents which are highly useful to society, such as the ability to do mathematics or engineering, (b) talents which are not particularly useful in the ordinary sense, although they give pleasure to others as well as to the possessor, such as the ability to make music or to paint, and (c) talents which do not seem to be socially useful at all, though not socially harmful either, such as the ability to play a good game of chess. No doubt the provision for (a) is chiefly motivated by the thought of utility, but the provision for (b) is made primarily, and for (c) wholly, because the possessors of talents obtain enjoyment and self-fulfilment from the development and exercise of them. Flutes or music scholarships are provided by public authority for those who can use them, not in order to give the populace the pleasure of future concerts, but in order that individuals with talent may obtain the happiness and self-fulfilment of using their talent. If the talent is a socially useful one, so much the better, and then the claim of utility is added to the claim of individual potentiality. If the talent is a socially harmful one, the claim of utility overrides the claim of individual potentiality. If the talent is neither useful nor harmful, its claim stands as a claim that has nothing to do with social utility and yet has a place in the scheme of equity.

The claim of ability is different from that of merit, since a man is not responsible for his abilities or disabilities and cannot strictly be said to deserve the benefits or burdens which they are apt to bring him. When we say that the most talented performer in a competition merits the prize, there is an element of desert proper, since talent must be matched by effort, for which the performer is responsible. Sometimes, however, as in a beauty contest, there is no question of effort but only of good fortune in natural endowments. We may still say that the winner 'merits' the prize, meaning simply that since a 'contest' (in fact, a comparison) in beauty has been set up and since this candidate is the most beautiful, she ought to be given the prize. This use of 'merit' and 'contest' is parasitic on the primary use, which refers to effort and its due reward.

As with ability, the claims of merit are most readily acknowledged when the meritorious achievement is socially useful. 'Merit awards' for industrial products are patently of this character. Effort in itself is not necessarily meritorious, and no rewards will be given to a man who works himself to the bone on a thoroughly useless occupation, such as digging holes for the sake of filling them in again. The Utilitarian seems to be on pretty strong ground when he argues that the claim of merit depends on utility. What counts is not simply useful consequences in the particular case but the usual tendency of the kind of effort expended. In a particular instance a man may be lucky and reap a rich harvest with little effort. In another instance he may be unlucky and find that hard work leads to no valuable result. Society often judges by actual and not merely probable results, just as its criminal law punishes more severely the evil intention which is followed by evil consequences than the evil intention which fortunately miscarries. Yet it will be agreed that merit and demerit depend on intention and effort rather than actual consequences. The Utilitarian accounts for this by reminding us that in general a man is more likely to produce a good or bad consequence by intention and effort than by chance, and that it is intentions and efforts which can be influenced by reward and punishment.

Even with merit, however, where the utilitarian case is most persuasive, the claim of equity does not always coincide with that of social utility. The merit of industriousness can, I think, be treated as wholly utilitarian, but not the merit of moral endeavour. To the extent that moral virtues are social virtues, one can say that the praise given to moral endeavour depends on its general tendency to benefit society. This can certainly be said of benevolence, which is always directed towards the good of others, and it can also be said of most instances of other moral virtues such as courage, honesty, and conscientiousness. There are times, however, when praise for these virtues is not connected with benefit to society but simply expresses the idea that they exhibit human excellence; and this must always be true of praise for the virtue of self-respect. Just as the claim of talent includes a claim for specifically human potentiality on its own account, so the claim of merit includes a claim for specifically human achievement on its own account.

The conclusion that merit and its due reward or praise cannot always be bound up with social utility is confirmed if we look at the other side of the coin, demerit. The punishment or blame that is deserved may be less, or more, than that which utility prescribes. To follow the rule of utility rather than that of desert strikes us as inequitable when the result is to deal with an offender more severely than he deserves, though not when the result is to deal with him more leniently. As we saw in Section 1, 'exemplary' punishment that goes beyond desert is warranted by utility but conflicts with equity. On the other hand, to lighten or waive deserved punishments that would do no good, is not felt to be a breach of justice. For example, one may think that a man who has deliberately taken the life of another *deserves* to lose his own life, but that the death penalty ought not to be used because it is not an effective deterrent. Then the abolition of the death penalty because it serves no useful purpose means that deliberate murderers are punished less severely than they deserve, but it would be absurd to say that abolition is unfair or unjust (presumably to the murderer's victim or else to previously executed murderers).

Since justice protects the rights of the individual as well as the order of society, justice and social utility can conflict as well as coincide. Of course, rights relate to essential interests, and the interest of society is made up of the interests of its members, so that justice and utility may be said to concern the same sort of ends. But because in practice 'the interest of society' has to mean the interest of the majority, there is a tendency for the interests of minority groups and of particular individuals to go by the board if we concentrate our attention upon securing the general interest; and we are apt to forget that 'the general interest' acquires its value only from being made up of the interests of individual persons. The concept of justice helps to remind us that all social values depend ultimately on our valuation of individual personality with its needs, desires, and enjoyments, its potentialities, aims, and achievements.

INDEX